STORIES OF BLACK FEMALE IDENTITY IN THE MAKING

Dr Kadian Pow

STORIES OF BLACK FEMALE IDENTITY IN THE MAKING

Queering the Love in Blackness

The Black Studies Collection

Collection editor
Dr Christopher McAuley

LPp

First published in 2023 by Lived Places Publishing

The authors and editors have made every effort to ensure the accuracy of information contained in this publication, but assume no responsibility for any errors, inaccuracies, inconsistencies and omissions. Likewise, every effort has been made to contact copyright holders. If any copyright material has been reproduced unwittingly and without permission the Publisher will gladly receive information enabling them to rectify any error or omission in subsequent editions.

British Library Cataloguing in Publication Data
A CIP record for this book is available from the British Library
9781915271471
ISBN: 9781915271457 (pbk)
ISBN: 9781915271471 (ePDF)
ISBN: 9781915271464 (ePUB)

The right of Kadian Pow to be identified as the Author of this work has been asserted by them in accordance with the Copyright, Design and Patents Act 1988.

Cover design by Fiachra McCarthy
Book design by Rachel Trolove of Twin Trail Design
Typeset by Newgen Publishing UK

Lived Places Publishing
Long Island
New York 11789

www.livedplacespublishing.com

Abstract

How does the concept of love fit with Black identity? This book is an exploration of the issues raised by this radical question—a refusal to center Black identity on whiteness; a question of how love, and self-love, fit with Black identity; and a queering of how Black identity is understood. Told through autobiographical reflection, this book contains the story of one Black woman's process of iterative identity formation, grappling with the intersections of sexuality, gender, self-image, and love. Focusing on lived experience, the book places theories in context, exploring what ideas look like when applied to real life, making it an invaluable reading for Black Studies and related courses.

Key words

intersectionality; African-American studies; Afro-Caribbean; LGBT+; femininity; lived experience; autobiography; sociology; race; gender

To my wife, Gillian, for loving me, for seeing me. I could not have finished this book without you.

To my grandmother, Elizabeth, for knowing when to pull me close and when to let me find my way. I really like who I am, and a big part of that is you.

To Kingston, Jamaica and Washington, DC, for inscribing a strong sense of racial identity.

To Bobigny and Livvie, for the cuddles and licks on the nose when I most needed them.

To the Vendée coast of France, for providing the peace, serenity, and sunshine that helped me let go and let the words flow.

Notes on language

Jamaican patois, as a form of vernacular English native to the author, is used sparingly across several chapters in this book. Sometimes as a word, a phrase, or section of dialogue, wherever it appears, the intention is to convey a cultural layer of meaning for which standard English is insufficient. Wherever patois appears as a word or phrase, standard English translation appears in parentheticals. When it appears as dialogue, the paragraphs that follow will provide context to help the reader understand, but not a word-for-word translation.

African-American Vernacular English (AAVE), also used sparingly throughout the chapters, follows much in the same way as the appearance of patois. There are no parenthetical translations, but endnotes will sometimes provide more context.

The lack of direct translation for both forms of Black vernacular English is intentional, but none of the language is difficult to decipher.

Contents

Learning objectives   xiii

Introduction   1

Chapter 1 Welcome to America   7

Chapter 2 Learning to be Black and female: an American dilemma   15

Chapter 3 Black liberation, who? Black liberation, what?   35

Chapter 4 White supremacy is whack   51

Chapter 5 Ex-church girl   67

Chapter 6 Sex and the Black Christian girl   83

Chapter 7 The road to Queerville   103

Chapter 8 Love as a mission   123

Notes   139

Discussion questions   145

References   147

Recommended further reading   151

Index   153

Learning objectives

1. To explore the ways in which Black identity is shaped by the confrontations between societal forces and domestic forces.

2. To grapple with how whiteness and feminism interact to produce exclusion.

3. To consider how the messages of Christianity pervade societal institutions and make it easier to internalize harmful concepts like sexual shame, patriarchy, and white authority.

4. To examine sexuality as a complex spectrum which can be affected by many factors, not just genetics.

5. To consider the contours of love and how we apply its practice outside of romantic encounters.

Introduction

If I didn't define myself for myself, I would be crunched into other people's fantasies for me and eaten alive.

Audre Lorde

I often tell my students that the concept of intersectionality existed long before Kimberlé Crenshaw (1991) gave life to it as a legal and analytical framework. Her work has benefited scholars who have come after her, including me. But Crenshaw's writings give us better insight into past voices, like Audre Lorde, who, through her writings, speeches, and activism, was mapping the margins long before "intersectionality" could roll off our tongues. In the same speech from which the opening quote is drawn, Lorde (1982) says, "There is no such thing as a single-issue struggle because we do not lead single-issue lives". Intersectionality tries to illuminate exactly that: race, gender, sexuality, class, and more do not function in separate silos; they co-mingle in complex ways to produce discrimination and privilege. But it is important to understand that behind these big concepts are people whose lives and identities are determined by sociological forces as well as through self-determination. The former can shape the latter.

Lorde defined herself by several terms, each flowing meaningfully into the next: Black, lesbian, mother, warrior, poet. There is no "and" at the end because those terms co-exist; they are not in hierarchy. She arrived at these descriptions after struggle and joy, learning what to keep and what to discard along the way.

Most importantly, she learned "to hold onto all the parts of me that served me, in spite of the pressure to express only one to the exclusion of all others" (Lorde, 1982). The right to maintain that complex identity was not a solipsistic striving. She put that complexity into her writing and speeches, which live on for our benefit.

I am not comparing myself to Audre Lorde, but you should know she has inspired my approach to this book. The journey to define myself found in the chapters you will read aims to elucidate how race, gender, sexuality, immigration, religion, and love function in the lived experiences of one person.

This book is not representative of *the* African-American woman's experience. First, I do not identify as African-American, preferring the expansiveness of "Black" instead. It leaves room for me to be both Jamaican and Black American. You will most frequently see "Black" instead of "African-American" in this book for that reason. You will read how both cultures impact my identity and perspectives differently at times. In fact, this book is not the definitive anything. Much like how in the brilliant *A Black Lady Sketch Show*, the "A" is doing a lot of work. This book represents *a* story, and *a* perspective on how Black identity is shaped. Its contents are defined as much by the experiences I had to exclude as the ones I did include. Oh, the stories that could fill another book! Be it the Tumblr essays about the TV show *Scandal* I used to churn out regularly[1] or the fiction I write, my observations and experiences have always implicitly informed my work. This book gives me the opportunity to make explicit connections between lived experiences and academic concepts that can sometimes feel slippery to grasp in authentic ways. I am an ethnographer, but I have written this more like memoir, dappled with sociological insights. The poet turned writer and mental health advocate Bassey Ikpi (2019) excavated her life to bring readers an understanding of living with bipolar disorder. She does so with beautifully wrought prose that is, at once, explicitly honest and protective; protective of her memories and the people in them, knowing that what she crafted for us to digest is the truth as she remembers, but, possibly, also a lie. We are only seeing through her lens. Our memories stitch together narratives from puzzle pieces, attempting to make sense of what we've been through. And so it is with this book.

Chapter 1: Welcome to America

My mother and I moved to the United States from Jamaica, to join the rest of our family who had been living in Washington DC for two years. The ways in which their Caribbean cultural attitudes would shape my perception of myself begin to unfold.

Chapter 2: Learning to be Black and female: an American dilemma

A Black woman is what I am, but not something I always understood how to be. Anyone who is Black in America must learn what such an identity is and how it is perceived in the wider, non-Black society. First, I write about what that was like coming to the USA as a non-American Black person, being shaped by 1980s and 1990s Washington, DC. Second, I talk about learning to be authentic to my own blackness when choosing which university to attend.

Chapter 3: Black liberation, who? Black liberation, what?

This chapter considers some of the external and internal barriers to feeling liberated as a Black person. I explore some unpopular reflections on the Black diasporic adage, "twice as hard for half as much!" What are the effects of internalizing this message, and are we prepared to confront the cultural shame we have absorbed from a racist society? Is the prospect of excellence always worth the leaning in, or is it more valuable to lean back for our own good?

Chapter 4: White supremacy is whack

"Woman" is not a universal category because of all the other intersecting identities that impact our experiences. Whiteness is something that often goes unacknowledged in feminist spaces, which is to say they ignore intersectionality. But its influence on what it means to identify and live as a woman is pervasive. This chapter considers my friendships with white women after the election of Donald Trump, and reflections on the patriarchy with which Sheryl Sandberg's "lean in" concept is painted. I offer an alternative.

Chapter 5: Ex-church girl

Named after the Beyoncé song "Church Girl", this chapter tackles evangelical Christianity and the sexual shame Black girls learn to absorb about their bodies, and the guilt that pleasure brings. How are these messages re-inscribed by our educational institutions? I detail what prompted my salvation at age twelve, and the doubt that plagued my ten years as a committed Christian.

(Content Warning: This chapter briefly mentions sexual assault. It does not render assault in drawn-out, graphic ways.)

Chapter 6: Sex and the Black Christian girl

Growing up deathly afraid of getting pregnant, especially because of the history of my family and the socio-political context of the 1990s Washington, DC, sex was something I obsessed over but avoided engaging in with another person. Christianity's influence on this cocktail of fear and fascination is explored. Understanding what it means to be attractive and feel attracted to someone is a lesson I outline based on several stories. It is something I wish was more explicitly discussed with all genders, but especially girls, because it empowers their bodily autonomy. Their bodies belong only to themselves.

Chapter 7: The road to Queerville

In this chapter, I discuss experiences in therapy and how my mental unwellness, at times, was an indication of avoidance. Without therapy, I may never have allowed myself to embrace queerness. I discuss my understanding of the difference between "queer" and "bisexual", as well as sexual identity as a spectrum. I also touch upon the nerdy story of meeting my now-wife in an online fan forum, and how we had to escape the United States to stay together.

Chapter 8: Love as a mission

In this final chapter, I explore my love of "love" in various forms, and talk about it as a practice we can apply. The focus on romantic applications is but one story of love. As a more experimental chapter, I navigate how love is an essential part of blackness, even when there is personal and communal trauma. I consider, too, as the founder of a hair-care brand for Black people, the question of whether love can meet capitalism, or whether the ghost of bell hooks is shaking her head at me.

(Content Warning: This chapter briefly mentions sexual assault. It does not render assault in drawn-out, graphic ways.)

Whatever your questions or rebuttals to what I have written, I hope it is useful to your understanding and to your life.

1
Welcome to America

My mother and I sat in the back of my grandparent's grey Nissan Sentra on a gloomy day, in late April of 1986. I stared out the window as we crossed over the 14th Street bridge, which served as the connection between northern Virginia and downtown Washington, DC. After being left behind for two years in Jamaica, my mother and I were finally reunited with my grandparents. I listened as the adults talked and I looked out the window at the cheerless landscape of the home of the brave and land of the free. Maybe America would prove magical, as I had repeatedly heard and intuited from the comments of adults around me in Jamaica. Even those who had never placed a toe on its soil spoke of the USA as full of promises they could never hope to hold in a land like Jamaica. "Foreign" (a vernacular term we used to refer to more prosperous countries) had transformed my grandparents' economic circumstances in just two years of Reagan-era America. The barrel full of pretty dresses grandmother sent to Jamaica for me was evidence to my childish brain of her much improved circumstances. But travelling in the back of their shiny new Nissan proved to me things were even better than I thought. Their car was far more impressive than the drab, mostly red brick buildings of post-riots, pre-gentrified downtown DC. My grandmother, as if reading my mind, recalled when she made this same trip in December 1983, in the back of her sister-in-law's car. "Is this it?" she had said back then. The cold water of reality splashed onto her myth-filled expectations on the day she, too, had arrived in this place. She was unimpressed, to say the least.

But I was impressed. Not by the city whirring past my window, but by the house on Longfellow Street that my grandparents had managed to purchase and completely furnish in the last year. It continues to be a common custom for immigrant families to practice strategic, phased resettlement in better economies. It is more feasible to "make a way" with fewer responsibilities in tow. Considering that they had been in America only two years, and with two children in tow, their house was significantly more impressive to me than any pile of red bricks downtown. The bricks on this 1930s colonial-style, four-bedroom row house were the color of dirty sand, like beach mixing with surrounding soil. There was a front garden full of roses and African violets, a small lawn, and a porch.

My mother's two younger sisters opened the door to us. Having received the tour of the house and settled into the small, pink front bedroom I would share with my youngest aunt (a three-year-old who could not wait to show me her collection of dolls), food was my next concern. I have loved food for as long as I can recall. A dark, lanky, almost seven-year-old taking in the surroundings of her new digs, my stomach roared. Assertively, I asked "Is wha fi dinnah?" The answer was curried goat with goonguh (pidgeon), peas, and rice, in honor of our arrival. I was beyond pleased to be the inspiration for the menu; enough that I had to let them know that they met my expectations by announcing immediately:"Ahohh, because mi nuh too too like di American food". The laughter that filled the vestibule and kitchen spaces was hearty and long. Coming from a child, this was funny. But it was made hilarious by the fact that I had never had American food in my short little life. Fast food was not as readily available in Kingston[2] in the 1980s as it is now, nor was it affordable, so I was deprived of the right to authentically judge American food. A minor detail. What I had gleaned from adults around me was that American food was not high-quality food; it was junk and inferior to the nutritious food we ate in Jamaica. I can understand now that my sense of relief about the dinner menu espoused a fear that my family had become "Americanized" and alien to me. Knowing that, despite the distance of the last two years, culturally, we were united about dinner gave me solace. Food assuaged my anxiety that day, and would continue to be a reoccurring theme as I adapted to my new home.

The smell of a Red Delicious apple will always take me back to 1986. It was early autumn, and displayed prominently in the entrance to the Safeway grocery store were wooden barrels of Red Delicious apples. Fragrant, shiny, waxy. It was my first trip to an American grocery store, and I begged my grandmother to put several of these pretty little things in her cart, and she indulged me. Though Red Delicious is a mealy-fleshed, woody, tasteless embarrassment to apples everywhere, the site of them will always conjure warm feelings. That apple-filled memory has set the tone for seven-year-old me, and life in America: encountering enticing products and people, many of which, when stripped back and experienced, turned out to be nothing of the sort. They were attractive, but ultimately disappointing. But also, food.

These memories mark the beginning of my lifelong obsession and battle with food.

Because we were not Americans, the Safeway grocery store was only the first stop in our food shopping adventure. Our Jamaican tastes and cravings required that we make at least one or two more stops to complete the weekly list of provisions. Mr. Blake's small Jamaican storefront had most of the necessary home goods— from goat meat to tins of Milo and, my favorite, sweetened tamarind balls. Grandmother would scoff at Mr. Blake's prices for fresh Caribbean produce like yellow yam, green pumpkin, white sweet potatoes, and so on. Eventually, she found better value at Red Apple Market, in immigrant-heavy Langley Park, Maryland, for non-American produce. This Chinese-run (back then) food emporium oddly enough specialized in African, Latin-American, and Caribbean foods, with a smattering of Chinese items. The store accurately reflected the people surrounding it. I looked forward to food shopping trips with my grandmother. Grocery stores are packed with cultural information about countries and their people—their tastes, their habits, and their values. I begin with food because it became representative of what I would choose to embrace as I decided what parts of America I wanted to drop into my identity basket, and to which parts from home I would cling. For me, these trips were part of shaping my American identity whilst always tethering me to the home I had left in Jamaica. Food was that throughline, which was established the day I arrived in America.

Finding that comfort, that sense of identity, grew more complicated in the subsequent months of settling into my new American life. I had left the first grade early in Jamaica and would have to sit out the rest of the spring and summer before attending my local elementary school. Luckily, I was smart enough to test into the second grade without having finished the first. Not exactly a major feat, but I was happy to be the same age as my peers in second grade. Having an accent and repeating the first grade would have been detrimental to my social life.

Almost the second I arrived on Longfellow Street that first day, my family accosted me with comments about how dark I had become. What happened to the brown skinned girl they left behind? The cool-toned[3] five-year-old featured in the picture whose milk-chocolate-colored face matched her tan and brown school uniform? The seven-year-old was standing in front of them as they waxed about the version of me in the picture. They remarked how mahgah (meagre, skinny) and dark I now was. This was not said in an abusive or dismissive manner but, instead, in a teasing way that I later understood to be a not-always-welcomed hallmark of many Caribbean cultures. The sort of talk that seems casual to the people saying it, but can get internalized by young minds, developing into traumas they only begin to unpack in their thirties, if they are able to afford therapy. Sometimes. For some. At that age, I did begin to internalize my family's comments about my appearance. After a few months, the extra-bronze veneer of the Jamaican sun began to fade due to all the time I spent indoors, especially since I didn't attend school for four months. As the brown skin they remembered returned, their color commentary waned. But a latent anxiety about my weight began to build. I knew by Jamaican standards that being mahgah was not good, and that I needed to find a remedy.

One day, I announced I was going on a diet. That's right, a diet. My seven-year-old understanding of that word was the polar opposite of what it meant. What I knew was that every commercial I saw whilst watching *All My Children* and *General Hospital* with my grandmother (she worked evenings) in which the word "diet" was used always contained food. People, predominantly white women, were always eating! I reasoned that to diet meant making an effort to eat more food. Never a picky eater, I was simply going to make eating a more consistently focused effort. I launched my first self-improvement campaign (how very American of me!) that summer of 1986. Little did I know that this "improvement" would lead to a steady, unceasing weight gain that eventually topped out at 238 pounds by age fourteen in 1993. Thereafter, a slow, jagged pendulum swing between "fit" and "extra thick" would plague me into my forties. The comments on my body never stopped, no matter how much or how little it was padded.

In 2023, my body is still a topic of conversation whenever I visit my family (now yearly, on account of my move to the UK). I'm now so familiar with their comments that I can anticipate what they will say depending on what I see in the mirror. The more visible my collarbones are, the less satisfied my grandmother is with my appearance. But the more satisfied I am. The two of us are like emotional seesaws when it comes to my appearance, in that the two of us cannot be happy at the same time about the way I look. If I am slightly uncomfortable with the upward trajectory of my weight, it is cause for grandmother to celebrate. The rest of my family sing a version of her song. The state of a female family member's body as a communal topic of conversation is not unique to my Jamaican family, or many non-European cultures. But just because something is part of one's culture, that does not make it inherently right or good, and certainly not easy to eradicate. Men's bodies belong to them; women's bodies belong to everyone except them, as if they are community property upon which everyone can place their mark in figurative and literal senses. Unless their bodies misalign with their gender identities, we do not make legislation denying men full ownership of their bodies.

In today's often black and white discourse about weight, it would be tempting to say that my family gave me a complex about my body. That they made me feel unattractive and were negligent of the ways in which I began developing an unhealthy relationship with food. That's a Twitter thread I am not compelled to write, even after several long-term bouts of therapy. The story is much more complicated than my seven-year-old or even fourteen-year-old brain could comprehend. But I internalized the complexity, even if subconsciously so. I don't entirely hate my body being under the spotlight of my family's gaze. Sometimes it feels good, affirming, energizing. But when my self-identity is fragile their opinions are harder to digest. The rare times my sense of self is aligned with their comments are enough to make me reluctant to banish the comments. I'm a vain, complicated person, OK?

Beyond vanity, here's the truth: the same extended family that pointed out my climbing weight repeatedly told me how beautiful I was; how ideal my brown color was; how shapely my figure was (once puberty hit). All of it was enough for me to grow as a confident girl who, though overweight, was beautiful, smart, *loving* and protected. I still wonder if, had I not been exposed at such a vulnerable age and during such a vulnerable time of cultural transition (having left my school, friends, and paternal family), food would have become a vehicle for my feelings, a way to focus my mind and shut out the other uncertainties of my life. How would I make new friends? What about my lingering accent? Would the American school make me repeat first grade? Would I ever understand this country and my place in it?

2
Learning to be Black and female in America

Black faces in white spaces

No one is born "woke". The making and re-shaping of ourselves, as we gain knowledge and experience, is a lifelong effort that some of us undertake with more intention than others. Understanding my own place within blackness—as a woman, as a queer person, and as a non-American Black—has been a long, ongoing process. I was a teenager before I truly began to understand "Black" as a sociological concept interpolated from the outside-in. In fact, whether because I was too young to comprehend or because my early years were spent in a nation of folks who looked like me, "Black" was something I learned in America: to be Black, and to understand its perception by others. My world had been so heavily centered around Black people up until that point that it did not occur to me to question myself as different or that I was seen as subordinate to white people (in some cases, other people of color, too). It took time to understand.

My primary and secondary public school education was at institutions consisting almost entirely of Black pupils and mostly

Black teachers. All of them were led by Black women principals. Black women being in charge was the default, and this was reinforced at home through my grandmother. Even though my grandfather sat at the head of the table and got the big piece of chicken, she was the true authority figure. This was Washington, DC in the late 1980s and 1990s, when Black people could still afford home ownership before Mayor Anthony Williams began actively courting gentrification in the early 2000s;[4] a city before Michelle Rhee became Chancellor of DC public schools and it became popular to remake public schools into charter schools foregrounding corporate agendas. Washington, DC is a very international city, but it is not cosmopolitan in the way that New York or London are. Its residential areas are largely racially segregated, and the relentless gentrification of the last twenty years did not alter this significantly. As a child there, I lived in a Black neighborhood on the Black side of northwest DC. My elementary school education emphasized repeatedly that America was a "melting pot". We were all just a big ol' stew of one assimilated American culture, ostensibly race-less but in practice very white. Besides TV, my encounters with white people did not happen regularly enough to make a difference in my life, or for me to be conscious of their impact on society and the way the world worked. My grandparents did not give me a talk about whiteness because it was not consequential to their upbringing in rural Jamaica. I was Black as a matter of living, being, breathing. It is how others perceive said blackness that I have had to contend with. As W.E.B. Dubois famously noted in *The Souls of Black Folk* (1903), this sense of "two-ness", or double consciousness, is a peculiar and dogged sensation that follows the American Negro as one strives to be the truest version of one's self.

In high school, my world became whiter, a little more multicultural. After allegations of fraud and sexual impropriety were levelled at the (newish) pastor of the long-time Church of God my grandparents and I attended, we fled that den of controversy. Grandmother's soul was unsettled there. One Sunday after I quit that church, my younger aunt and I were ushered off to a suburban church in neighboring Maryland. Our former storefront church was also in Maryland, but in Prince Georges County— the Black county. This new church was in Rockville, Maryland, squarely in one of the wealthiest (whitest) counties in the nation: Montgomery County. Its suburban setting, white pastor, and First Lady choir director of the church were very new to me. This shift would mark my first time being under institutional white authority. But the congregation was not entirely white, just majority white. Other Jamaicans had flocked there, too, including a couple who also fled our former scandal-ridden church. To my surprise, there were also a fair number of Filipinos. It was at this church that, for the first time, I saw interracial dating in real life and gained non-Black friends. Elementary school had been my first introduction to American blackness and the expectations it had of me to fit in. I watched a lot of television and was generally aware of racial dynamics, but it wasn't until I attended the Rockville church that I gained an intimate view of how Black was perceived by non-Black people, both the white ones and other people of color. Each group had their own expectations, assumptions, and blinders that were specifically shaped by an American mythology of Black people as deficient humans.

The Rockville church enjoyed shouting its multicultural credentials from its pulpit and at its regional and national church conferences. Like any corporate entity, all denominations of American churches have corporate structures resembling private enterprises, despite their tax-free status. As such, their power and authority positions were concentrated among the same types of people: white ones. This is an example of the ways in which we often mistake diversity for equality. They are not synonyms for each other. Diversity is the seasoning one adds after the meal is cooked to add a little extra flair or enhance the taste. Equality is the foundation of the recipe, without which the meal is fundamentally altered. A character in a Ryan Murphy show once expressed the difference perfectly: "You wanted a Black face, not a Black voice![5]" A face represents presence; a voice represents potential power.

What your college choice says about your blackness

University was a very exciting and anxiety-inducing prospect for me as a teenager. I attended a "Blue Ribbon"[6] School, Benjamin Banneker Academic Senior High School. The emphasis on "academic" meant it was not a neighborhood feeder school. Students from all over DC were allowed to apply, so long as they met the entry requirements: a minimum 3.0 GPA, lengthy application, placement exam, interview, and recommendation letters. This place treated high school like it was already college. I was accepted, but on the condition that I attended their Summer Institute ahead of starting ninth grade. My math scores were … not great, and I was also on the lower end of a 3.0 GPA. To be fair, I only began treating school seriously in the eighth grade after a rudderless seventh-grade year. I knew Banneker would put me on the disciplined path needed to attend university. I was determined to realize at least this much of the "American Dream".

It is very common for Black people with at least one university degree to embrace a good old-fashioned polemic debate on Twitter. Which type of institution is the better educational and emotional fit for Black people: a Historically Black University or College (HBCU), or a Predominately White Institution (PWI)? As an aside, I wish we referred to the latter as Historically White Institutions (HWIs) because that is what they are. Their majority white status is a result of centuries-old deliberate practice of racial exclusion or unfair criteria for Black admittance. This rigid adherence to white supremacy left Black people no other option but to create their own institutions of higher education.

Nevertheless, the cyclical, racialized arguments about university degrees that take place on social media tend to be flat, reducing culture to familiar tropes that reflect surface level experiences at higher learning institutions. Folks debate which type of institution could guarantee better financial outcomes for graduates, better supportive environments for Black people, and better professional networks. These arguments invariably dredge up debates around Black cultural authenticity: are those who attend PWIs hungry for white validation? What about the chronic under-funding of HBCUs which makes it harder for them to compete on the same level as some private PWIs? Both questions are indicative of two ends of the systemic economic equality spectrum.[7] The overall level of funding Harvard receives is profoundly different from its HBCU equivalent, Howard.

This section is not about regurgitating those kinds of polemic debates, nor am I here to make definitive closing arguments on behalf of one or the other institution. Because, ultimately, I don't have the power to decide anything except for how I relay my own experience as one Black person choosing between an HBCU and a (H)PWI. The needless back and forth online is just a form of entertainment. The litany of 280-character posts rarely reflects the complex or stark honesty (scholarship money) behind the decision process of choosing (if one even has a choice) a university. What I can talk about is having a pretty great Black experience at a small PWI, and what led me away from choosing an HBCU.

My first set of college visits took place in the spring of 1995, my sophomore year of high school. Via chartered bus, we visited a handful of HBCUs during spring break: from Hampton, Virginia to Atlanta, Georgia. There are HBCUs in plenty of other states (including my home state-in-bondage, Washington DC). But Banneker was across the street (literally) from Howard University's main campus. By sophomore year, when the trip was to take place, we were overfamiliar with Howard, thus it was scrapped from the official itinerary. We knew it was prestigious and had a long history of excellence, but it was also the place where many students did the volunteer hours that were required before graduation. Howard's Blackburn ballroom held our annual Winter Ball, not to mention every Banneker graduation each June. We were teenagers and Howard was too close for us to dream about or lust after. It was not the coveted Hillman University[8] experience we grew up idolizing whilst consuming Lisa Bonnet and Cree Summer's college antics on the TV show *A Different World*. Many of us longed to get away from home, for was that not the quintessential college experience? At least, that is what

I pictured in my head. Being away from home, living in a dorm, toting a shower caddy to and from the bathroom, complaining of cafeteria food with people who would become lifelong friends. I could not wait. I did not even bother applying to schools to which I could commute from my house. I recognize that the "away" experience of college is a privilege for some, as living at home and commuting to a community college or in-state university system is a better (and smarter) financial proposition for most, but that is the adult version of myself looking back with hindsight and remaining student loans. The debt-free teenage girl that I was, dreamed of campus life and nothing else would do.

Two white teachers (and co-sponsors of the class of 1997), Dave and Matt, were the lead chaperones for our HBCU tour. We began with Virginia-based Hampton University and eventually concluded in Atlanta with Spellman and Morehouse colleges, along with Clark Atlanta University (where my ex-fiancé attended—more on that later). Banneker had an interesting setup wherein each class chose two teachers to sponsor our activities and trips. We chose the young, "cool" instructors. Dave and Matt were basketball heads, and following a visit to Fayetteville State University, when the basketball-obsessed boys in our class begged to stop at top-tier college sports institution (and PWI), University of North Carolina-Chapel Hill (UNC), they did not pretend to resist. One braces-faced kid, Brandon, got his dream fulfilled. "Jerry Stackouse!" he yelled, unforgettably, when he saw the UNC (and eventual college coach) basketball player that spring of 1995. I still remember how his voice cracked during that gleeful squeal.

The trip was a good time, and valuable in that I got a more realistic picture of what college campuses were like. I got to see people who looked like me taking up all sorts of academic and social interests. These were institutions where Black life was central and centered. I hate to count it as fortunate (but I do) that such a thing was not special to me because most of my existence by the age of fifteen was Black by default. I was not isolated in white suburbia, and therefore did not have to yearn for Black friends, or worse, be unconscious of such a need. The blackness of the universities was not a top selling point for me, but the location was. Black university life was my first encounter with collegiate culture. I focused on factors like academic programs, university size, cost, available scholarships. Then there was the intangible factor of how I felt on these campuses. How easy was it to envision myself blossoming there? I came away from the southern college tour with an incommunicable conviction that the southeast was not for me. By this, I mean the environmental and cultural ways of the South. The heat, too. None of it was for me, irrespective of the fun I had touring each campus. Visits to my older sister in her adopted state of Florida did not endear me to that state or the South as a region. Only folks north of Washington, DC like to throw the Mason-Dixon line (bordering Maryland, Pennsylvania, and Delaware), around as the official geographic, social, political, and cultural dividing line between the northeast and the south. But having lived in Washington, DC and Maryland, most residents there do not regard themselves as "southerners", and states south of DC do not regard us as such either. The DC area is a hodgepodge transitional space of transculturation, partly because, as the nation's political capital, it attracts people from all over the United States and around the world.

Living a Jamaican way of life at home and an African-American life at school, I had acculturated many parts of Black American culture. But going further south revealed to me a well of ignorance about Southern culture in which I, unfortunately, swaddled myself rather than remedied until later in life. In this way, it was easier to feel alienated down there than at home. My antipathy toward the South had been budding for years, starting with the neighboring state of Virginia. Ever since I learned that they rescinded the land they previously acquiesced to the capital, Washington, DC, I never looked at that state with neutrality. And, of course, Robert E. Lee, president of the Confederacy, hailed from Virginia, and the state continues honoring the legacy of this traitor with streets named after him, monuments, and buildings. In short, fuck Virginia. Safe to say, wrong or right, I already held a bias against Southern life even as I enjoyed its influence in my beloved Washington, DC. I know now that young me underplayed how much African-Americans had created what we culturally know as Southern American life—food, music, traditions, language, and more—which would go on to influence American culture writ large.[9] An older me grew to appreciate and take pride in that. But fifteen-year-old Kadian was culturally short-sighted. Much of that is because my education about the South focused on it as a place of Black people's subjugation rather than a place of cultural creation. My young brain could not hold a more complicated view, nor did I receive one. As people who grew up outside of the United States, I was not fortunate to have had these things passed down to me through family traditions. Though I have a better appreciation for the southeast now, including many visits to almost every state, I still have no interest in living there.

When applying to universities my senior year of high school, Pennsylvania was the "Southern"-most state to which I applied.

Vassar girl

I ended up attending a PWI; the exact one I eventually set my sights on a year after the "Southern Black College Tour", as it was dubbed. Black women were integral to my discovery of, visit to, and attending of Vassar College in Poughkeepsie, New York.

"I can see you at that kind of school, you know?" said my best friend, Melissa. It was autumn in the critical junior year of high school when we would take our college entrance exams; the year when one's cumulative GPA and SAT scores were most scrutinized.

"What school?" I replied, confused by her non-sequitur after asking me how I found the current book I was reading.

She pointed to the Danielle Steele (1989) novel in my hand, *Star*. "The heroine in the book you're reading. She went to Vassar, no? That's the kind of place that would suit you".

I was speechless, but also uncertain of whether to be flattered or insulted. In the novel, Elizabeth—the protagonist's' main competition for a man—is a refined socialite who attends Vassar College. I was no socialite, but did Melissa see me even in the vicinity of refinement?

When I looked at Melissa with great confusion and expecting a string of reasons to flow out of her mouth, she pushed up her glasses, shrugged her shoulders, and said: "I gave you that book because *Star* reminds me of you". For someone who so expertly wielded her vocabulary, she was short on words.

I knew nothing about the mid-Hudson River college except that its mention was synonymous with well-bred white girls who were looking to marry into social and economic security. What part of that made one Black girl recommend it to another? Melissa was even more reserved than I was, and was born in the United States to Caribbean parents, who I knew to be lovely and welcoming. They also kept an exceptionally neat home. Melissa was a prodigious reader and consumer of American politics. She demurred from public speaking, loved the TV show *Seinfeld* (as did I), and preferred understated versions of designer brands I could not afford. I let her convince me I was a Republican, though that was over and canceled by the time my father drove me through Vassar's gates. Later, as I grew to understand myself, I recognized that words are insufficient to communicate what she felt, which was an instinct; one that I was later convinced of, too. One that was right. Did I attend Vassar College because of a Danielle Steele novel? No. But did I research the college because Melissa, who knew me well, introduced its possibility to me? Absolutely.

My family could not advise me practically through this college application process, for neither my mother (who was in prison at this point), father (raising two children with his wife in Brooklyn), nor grandparents had been through this. Even my older cousins—the children of the great aunt who sponsored my grandparents to come to America—had not attended university. I looked to Banneker's high school guidance counsellors and other honor roll students for cues on how to proceed. Choosing a university was pitched as a major decision that would change the trajectory of my life. But how would I know if I had made the right decision?

I applied to Vassar and other liberal arts colleges, including Wellesley, Sarah Lawrence, and Oberlin. Big universities like Brown, Northwestern, and Drexel were also on my list. State universities were largely excluded from my list because, with few exceptions, I absorbed the elitism of my classmates, joining them in pooh-poohing state universities as unbefitting of a Banneker graduate. As a "safety school", state universities were fine. With this uninformedly discerning point of view, I applied to nearly a dozen universities. Doing so did not ding my family's pockets too badly because I secured application fee vouchers for the most expensive ones. Back then, fees ranged from $30 to $65 for each application, which were sent by old-fashioned mail. My grandmother did not tell me to pare down my list to lower the cost. Educational pursuit, in my family, received little budgetary scrutiny. Without batting a lash, we would be denied when lusting after clothes, shoes, a video game, or anything else deemed frivolous, but not when it came to the very thing my grandparents had brought their family to America to pursue. If it was "for school", it would receive budgetary approval. "Mi haffi find it" is a phrase my grandmother would often say when funds were needed but did not exist. To me, it was magic when money appeared when I needed it.

I didn't yet know there was an African American Alumni of Vassar College (AAAVC) organization. But when, in my senior year, I became aware of their existence and discovered their organization was sponsoring a weekend college visit to Vassar's campus for free, I jumped at the chance. A lot of colleges attempt to increase their "diversity" numbers by arranging college visits for potential applicants, during which the applicants are welded to the Black and POC college students who volunteer for the yearly farce. The hope is that the social interactions will serve as keen enticement for students to apply. This is not a wild departure from what took place on the HBCU campus visits, but the intent is different in that HBCUs were not trying to compensate for a racial absence on campus. The cynical part of me thinks that universities that are seen as "exclusive" want more applicants because then they can reject more of them, thus making their paltry acceptance rate stand out even more. The fewer people they accept, the more exclusive their reputation remains.

It is possible that the women who mostly comprised the AAAVC were being funded by Vassar itself to sponsor such trips in its diversity recruitment efforts, but at the time I was not cognizant of such politics, nor did the zeal of these women inspire discomfort or pressure during either bus ride between DC and Poughkeepsie. Later, when I became friends with an African-American alumnus of Sarah Lawrence College (an hour south of Vassar)—Yvonne, who is still very active with the college—I came to understand that the recruitment push at these East Coast PWIs were very political for the Black baby boomer generation. They had infiltrated these elite institutions as part of the civil rights wins in the 1960s and1970s, seizing their right to attend university in any state they pleased. It was that generation of Black people who took over buildings on campuses and fought hard battles for these universities to recruit Black professors, establish African-American study programs, Black Student Unions (BSU), and curb or end other hostile discriminatory practices. Increasing Black student enrolment at these PWIs was part of the legacy of what they had fought for; a kind of re-inhabitation of things previously denied to us.[10] I knew none of that then. But I did know those women represented the future of what I could be—successful, beautiful, supportive, Black. This history of Black activism at PWIs is part of what gets lost in the HBCU versus PWI discussions.

The weekend visit to Vassar went off without a hitch. I was assigned a "buddy", Janice, from the Bahamas. Having that Caribbean connection endured me to her instantly. I hung out with Janice and her small, diverse friend group—one other Black girl, an Indian Muslim, and a very short, funny white girl. All of them were from New York state and lived in the only all-female dorm on campus, Strong. After that weekend, it was easy for me to see myself there. And I did. I began having repeat visions of my life there, created by my subconscious, made conscious for me without much effort. I belonged at Vassar. Never did I doubt that I would be accepted, but paying for it caused me plenty of anxiety. Fortunately, I received a hardship scholarship that covered ninety percent of tuition and fees.

The Black Student Union at the college organized an orientation week for the students who identified themselves as Black on their applications. This took place the week before the official start of the fall term. Orientation week was not mandatory, but it was clear to me it would give me more of a chance to settle in and, maybe, make some friends. With fewer people that week it might be easier. My high school graduating class had eighty-seven students, all but four of them Black. The Black students in Vassar's class of 2001 were scarce by comparison.

Though a highly sensitive introvert, I did make plenty of friends. Whilst there was a strong presence of Black men in my class (including Shaka King, director of *Judas and the Black Messiah*

(2021)), the majority identified as women. That first week exposed me to so many types of blackness through these people: hardcore vegans, lesbians, bohemians, spoken-word poetry types who styled themselves like Erykah Badu, rock chicks, Goths, stoners, boarding school girlies, non-American Blacks, amalgamations of all of those, and much more. It made me giddy, this candy store of blackness. To think that people paint swaths of Black people who choose (or are compelled by circumstances) to attend PWIs with the same brush is not at all reflective of the actual experience of being there. I had a black ass time at very white Vassar College. This is not intended to negate the experiences of Black people who are stigmatized, racially subjugated, or experience forms of undue violence whilst attending a PWI. I am sharing my experience at Vassar as one that exposed for me how diverse American blackness was, especially among women-identified people.

Bouts of trauma and all, the undergraduate years of my life were significant in shaping my interests and who I would become. I fell in love with the subject of anthropology. I realized my dream of studying and traveling in India. I received years of free mental health therapy. I was loved. I was introduced to queerness from a Black feminine perspective. And so much more. Some of the friendships I made at Vassar endure as I write this. I was fortunate to have had a spectacular structure of Black and POC throughout my time there, all of which help me color that era in a rosy hue. Not long ago, I looked at pictures from graduation day and had two prevailing thoughts: (1) from those photos, it is hard to tell what a white-ass school it is, and (2) why did I let my mother convince me to wear that dress under my graduation gown? Too much cleavage.

Kentucky fried nope

My grandmother would constantly tell me to come and learn something from her in the kitchen. I will always remember Grandmother yelling, "Kady! Come learn fih cook!"

After all, how would I provide for myself and my husband? Did I expect Kentucky Fried Chicken to service those needs, she would joke. Then she would let out a hearty laugh at the ridiculous thought of me being dependent on fast food to nourish this imaginary husband (and children, presumably). "Oh, mama", I would say, barely drawing my eyes away from the TV in the adjoining den, lazy as ever. "I don't need to learn how to cook. I'm going to be rich, and I'll have someone take care of things like that".

When my grandfather died during my sophomore year of college, my grandmother stopped cooking on a daily basis. Her responsibilities to her husband had ended when his life did, including making daily family meals. Perhaps two or three times a week, she would produce a meal, including the all-important post-church Sunday meal, which began Saturday night with soaking the legumes for the "rice and peas" dish; she would also cook for special occasions like Thanksgiving and Christmas Day. Today, it is a rare treat for my grandmother to cook at all, mostly because a slipped disc in her spine makes it hard to stand for long periods of time. I was nineteen, away at university, and only home for brief breaks and summers. Grandmother's youngest (the aunt who is like a sister to me) was sixteen and pregnant with her first child. My older aunt was living in the house at the time with her son who was twelve. It was the time when everyone in the house started taking partial responsibility for themselves. I sometimes wonder if Grandmother would have felt compelled to keep cooking if she had had sons rather than daughters living with her. She never called my uncle to the kitchen to learn the vital adult skill of making food for oneself (which is never how cooking is introduced to girls). Or maybe one of the girls would have been asked to take up the duty on his behalf. This is an example of the different gendered expectations we place on children in the home. Instead of viewing cooking as a necessary life skill for all human adults to learn, it is often portrayed as a hetero-patriarchal skill girls must learn in order to perform for the future benefit of men and the families we will create with them.

I eventually did learn how to cook. I became interested when I moved to Madison, Wisconsin for my master's degree program (gasp! At a state school!). Living on my own, paying bills, and working part time, I quickly learned how much take-out emptied my pockets. I learned to cook from books, the internet, TV food programs, and yes, my grandmother. It was my first time being entirely independent. Because cooking was not a duty to anyone else, I began to embrace it as a creative outlet and budget-saving endeavor. I could not yet afford to go to Paris, but I could learn how to make coq-au-vin. Now, one of my greatest pleasures is cooking for me and my wife. Cooking is my love language, a way that I take care of my wife and pets (yes, I make food for them); it is a creative, de-stressing outlet for me. Those sentiments were not something I grew up attaching to food preparation in my household. I don't have to cook, but I love doing it, only partly because my wife enjoys my cooking and baking efforts. She is still imploring me to learn my grandmother's oxtail recipe. I hate to tell her that no matter what I do, my oxtail and butterbeans will never taste like hers because we don't do recipes and measurements. The ingredients are standard, but I will never possess Grandmother's panache in the kitchen, even if I had paid attention all those years ago.

I go home to DC every year. Because of the Covid-19 pandemic, I have not seen my grandmother and other family members since spring of 2019. In 2022, I made my own birthday cake as a gift to myself. I recognize that I can derive pleasure from it because it is not tied to obligation or economic constraint. Half of the three-layer chocolate cake with cookies and cream Italian meringue frosting that I made sits in my freezer. Soon, it will be transported, with me, to America so that Grandmother can taste what I have finally learned.

As we grow, learning what it means to be human, those of us born into female bodies are absorbing messages and projections from others about ourselves; so many messages that they can be overwhelming as we go through awkward adolescent years yearning to understand who we are. These messages are, invariably, laden with expectations we drag into adulthood. We learn early that a significant portion of our lives should be spent in service to a man, not as part of a shared sense of responsibility in a relationship, or as acts of love. No: this caretaker role, as an act of maintaining the patriarchal order, is told to and modelled for us from an early age so that it becomes *naturalized,* though it is not natural. We watch our mothers care for our fathers. If we have a younger brother, we are expected to help take care of him, too. As adult women, we are told our duty is to take care of the children we have with our chosen man, even when we, too, are breadwinners. If we are lucky enough to have geriatric parents, we are expected to take care of them also. These are examples of what sociologist Arlie Russell Hochschild (1989) terms the "second shift": an appropriation of labor terminology to emphasize the additional domestic labor expected of women once they finish their wage-earning jobs. Women's lifelong service to the family, especially for eldest daughters, only ceases when we die. Moreover, we are responsible for passing down these traditions, indoctrinating daughters, nieces, cousins, whilst also patrolling them to make sure everyone toes the patriarchal line.

The anxiety of impending adulthood

How to "do adulthood" filled me with significant dread and anticipation. I spent years rebuffing Grandmother's invitations to learn cooking because that skill did not seem to be high on the priority list of how to become an adult. Cooking was something I could pick up later, or outsource if necessary. Marrying a man and having children—in that order—seemed axiomatic to the adult female experience, as my not-quite-twelve-year-old brain rationalized. I was not anxious about performing those roles, approaching their inevitability with a limp shrug. But what kind of woman would I be? What career path would I follow? What cocktail of passion and drive would propel me toward success? These were the giant anxiety mosquitoes buzzing about my head.

I realized there were elderly and middle-aged women, outside of my family, who were untapped resources. They had been adulting since before I was born! I began tap-tap-tappin' that source as early as age twelve. Women at my church and my schoolteachers largely comprised my knowledge posse, but I took care to learn from those at my internships and mandatory volunteering[11] gigs all throughout high school, too. Central to what I wanted to know was how does one become who they are? This was an existential question I did not realize I sought to answer. Instead, I framed the question in terms of careers, foolishly under the misapprehension that what one did and who one was were one and the same. I was in my thirties before I understood this not to be the case. But living in Washington, DC for a significant portion of one's life can cause your understanding of career ambitions to become skewed. That city is full of ambitious, career-ladder-climbing types. I had more experiences than I can count of being asked for my name, immediately followed by the "and where are you?" question. This was not an existential prodding about where I was in my life's journey, but a literal question about the location of my employer. Because the answer would determine the rest of the conversation.

Older Black women were resources to me in a way I could only begin to comprehend once I was in the middle of adulthood. I just knew, back then, that they possessed the key to ushering me toward the vast, frightening land of grown-ness I would have to navigate. And though I still have many days in which I need an adult to pick me up off the ground, I think they prepared me pretty well.

3
Black liberation, who? Black liberation, what?

I developed an antipathy to middle-aged white men not long after coming to America. That early seed was sown by my grandmother, perhaps, without her truly knowing. The seeds of knowledge she dropped into the fertile soil of young Kadian's brain would, in a couple of decades, awaken her to understanding white supremacy on a structural, historical, and existential level. A kernel of truth inside a trite '90s joke was that white people (particularly women) would hastily cross the street whenever they saw a Black man. They assumed the worst because white people have internalized "Black" as a signifier for danger, and Black people as the embodiment of criminality. *Policing the Crisis: Mugging, The State and Law and Order*[12], by cultural theorist Stuart Hall (1982), painstakingly details the ways in which the relationship between state sanctioned law enforcement and media narratives work in support of exaggerating Black criminality to reinforce social order. It is both a conscious (though often denied) and subconsciously learned association that is reinforced through media representation, as well as through social circles. Take that stereotype but swap the races, and there you have young

Kadian's potent sense of unease. For me, it was middle-aged (and older) white men that represented the potential for danger and had a propensity toward villainy. At least that was my reading of media I consumed. This internalized fear has not completely dissipated, but I am cognizant about working through it. The older I become and the more experiences I collect, the lower the age threshold is for my wariness. White toddlers are the only ones around whom I will let down my guard. Slightly.

My grandmother understood from her short time in the USA that white people possess two faces. One, they use to treat you kindly so long as you "behave" and do not threaten their authority or place in the racial hierarchy. Then there is the other face that, should you displease or offend their societal perspectives, would easily discard you as if you were not a person. Grandmother worked for a health service business that provided in-home health aides and inpatient care for elderly persons. The majority of those receiving the care were white. I have never known mama to be uncivil to anyone, but she learned to protect her spirit at work. The way her beautiful smile lights up her coffee skin, her booming easy laugh, and her empathy: those she gave to her patients and their families. But they were not allowed to access a deeper sense of who she was, mostly because they revealed no genuine interest in her humanity. They needed her service, not her. In the forty years that my grandmother spent in that line of work, I have only known her to have one patient who truly cared about Elizabeth the person, and about her family at home. I am fortunate to have met him. Ah-lahv hashalom,[13] Mo.

Half-human with twice the stress

At some point, most Black children learn to de-center themselves around white people. We learn to split ourselves into two parts that many of us spend years trying to reconcile. Those parts consist of the part of us we had been growing to know and a stranger part that performs a version of us. To everyone else, that stranger becomes the stand-in for us, our avatar. It is an existential fight, as a Black person, to remember who you are in a society that willfully ignores you, preferring the performance of your avatar instead. Mostly, this is a stressful burden, but occasionally you can use the stranger as a puppet for defensive deception.

This two-ness, or double consciousness, as W.E.B. Du Bois calls it, begins when we learn a prevalent Black proverb: "You have to work twice as hard to get half as much". Perhaps I blocked it out, or maybe it was never said enough times to inspire anxiety, but that term is not something with which I grew up. It is not because I am Jamaican, because I know people from Caribbean families and Black folks in parts of the diaspora outside of America who have had this proverb drilled into their heads to the point of cliché. Yes, just paragraphs ago I opined learning early of white men's penchant for treachery, but being told I would be seen as half of who they are? That I was not told, and for that omission I am thankful. Reader, you may think that having half as much and being regarded as being half as much are two separate things. I assure you that in a country where one is the sum of their accumulated wealth and possessions, these things are one in the same. If white men are regarded as the pinnacle of humanity, laboring, as a Black person, to achieve superhuman capacity just to surround yourself with half the outcome is tantamount to being seen as half a human being. Why would I put in that much work just to be regarded in the exact same way as if I had done nothing?

Whilst I know this sentiment is not exclusive to Black culture(s), and that it resonates with people of color who are living in white-dominant, hetero-patriarchal societies the world over, Black people, especially African-Americans, have adopted the adage as their own because that is how they have experienced life in America. They have been looked upon as inhuman (at worst), secondary humans (at best). I grew up in a Jamaican household in a city heavily shaped by African-American culture: Washington DC, or "Chocolate City", as it was colloquially referred to back in the 1980s and 1990s. My northwest neighborhood, Brightwood, teemed with Black people, with a sprinkling of Latinos, mostly from Central America. Up until high school, my world was so dominated by multiple Black cultural influences that I took for granted that this was the case for everyone. We tend to be myopic when we are young because our sense of the world is just as small.

I am thankful I never had the opportunity to internalize the "twice as much" adage because, frankly, I despise it—as a record label and a crew. Yes, I know and understand very well that "you have to work twice as hard to get half as much (as them)" is imparted by families to their children to fortify them in a world fundamentally hostile to their existence; a world forcing them to play the game of life in "difficult mode" with fewer resources. It is a reality check and a stay against the inevitable onslaught of obstacles Black children do and will face. It's keeping it real. But sometimes keeping it real can go wrong. Reality is important for grounding us and keeping us safe, but it is limiting in the sense that its job is to reveal what directly confronts us. But it also obscures what can be possible. To paraphrase Toni Morrison (1994), the duty of racism (which is the root of "twice as much") is to keep us from dreaming, creating, doing, by making us limit ourselves. In some ways, drilling the "twice as much" adage into our children's heads is us doing free labor for racism. Twice the work for half the reward points only to sobriety, not possibility. The latter is my favorite word, and I don't know if it would have been if it was drilled into me that I had to work twice as hard to get half of something I wanted.

Trigonometry almost broke my brain. I used to be in the Math Honor Society in high school (yes, me, the girl who had to attend summer school to improve her math scores), but after barely making it through trigonometry, I tapped out after pre-calculus. But I know enough about numbers to know that the math is not mathing on the "twice as much" proverb. Twice my energy for little in return is unsustainable and a bad investment strategy for a long life. The world is going to end soon. I'd rather conserve my energy. I'd rather put in less effort to be content with my return rather than expending so much energy only to resent a meagre outcome. I'm only one human. I want to be careful to say that internalizing the twice as hard/half as much speech is not the fault of Black people. It is a coping device. Like most coping devices, it will never get to the root of the problem. We may not ever be able to completely overhaul white supremacy (that would actually require a massive amount of buy-in from white people, of which they are existentially allergic), but it is our responsibility to create a framework for life on our own terms.

Immigrant try-hard

It makes sense to me now that *my* Jamaican family never pushed the familiar adage on any of us, though plenty of others did. I also understand that my perspective is heavily influenced by my outsider-ness, a non-American blackness teetering on a fulcrum between the reality of America and the promises I was told it could bring. As the first grandchild in the family, born to a sixteen-year-old mother and thirty-four-year-old grandmother, I inhabited a strange space in the family, between child and grandchild. Jamaica is a class-based society where the legacy of British colonialism and its attendant European Christian influences of bigotry and color prejudice still reign. I grew up poor (which did resonate with me as a child), in a family of dark skin, working-class people trying to make ends meet. My grandparents' families before them were the same. My mom was forced to leave high school when pregnant with me and never went back.[14] Everyone else in the family ended their education after high school.

All this is being said to rationalize the following: my family did not believe in a mutable class framework which would allow them to climb to a station above what they had grown to expect. Not in Jamaica. Of course, this system is limiting and not one in which I would like to live. But because my parents and grandparents did not receive the half as much spiel, they focused on creating a life for themselves and their children, doing the best with what they had. They reached the so-called Land of Opportunity not because of hard work, which they certainly put in like a lot of other people, but because of some luck and a few family members who had reached the United States and then reached back to lend my grandparents a helping hand. The hard graft really came after they reached America's shores, and it has never let up.

My family did not cultivate American friends, sticking instead to networks of Caribbean acquaintances known through church, work, and family connections. Education had always been drilled into us as a kind of guide to a better life. By age five, I was reading independently, but the move to America made the education emphasis even stronger because, as my grandparents saw it, the opportunities were more plentiful. To not develop some ambition for ourselves would be a waste and a shame. I digested this because to be wasteful was a very bad thing, especially when you have so little to begin with.

I was by no means an intellectual phenom—not now and not then. But because my family's expectation was simply that I try my best and take advantage of opportunities to bring me success, most of my ambitious spirit was developed through external stimuli. Looking back, I didn't know then how good I had it. I moved from a Black country to a very Black American city (before it became the gentrified enclave it is now). I could have ended up somewhere shockingly white, like Kansas, or Vermont, and suffered an alienating experience. Or not. All three of the DC public schools I attended were at least ninety-five percent Black, and all of them were presided over by Black women principals. I had no reason to think this rare at the time. All three managed their schools similarly—with a stern glove that meted out consequences for disobedience, but also provided guidance whilst expecting students to do well.

The most impactful of these three women was Lynette Adams, former principal of Benjamin Banneker Academic Senior High

School. It was under her tutelage that I came to understand a greater capacity for the intelligence, effort, and achievement that I possessed, but had not tapped. Imposter syndrome was not a thing for me because Black excellence surrounded me at Banneker. This excellence, Mrs. Adams emphasized, was not about the grades we achieved, or the scholarships we collected, but who we were intrinsically. She protected our little souls and maintained an environment that was as competitive as it was affirming. She taught me that just because I was young, Black, and female did not mean that I was low on the priority list, unlike the messages we received from the wider world. She told us that we, the students, were her priority and that if we needed her, it did not matter if she was in a meeting. Our needs, if they required her input to be resolved, would be prioritized. The partner in the meeting would have to wait. I can attest to having witnessed her values in action.

The presumption at Banneker was that we were all bound for college, which included specialist art or design institutes. Regarded as a college preparatory high school, Banneker boasted a ninety-eight percent college acceptance rate. Those on the honor roll were a big deal in the school. They were stars. Being somewhat nerdy was required to apply to the school (a 3.0 GPA at a minimum). And because everyone was technically a nerd, you could also be popular, awkward, political, athletic, artsy, and so on. We were multi-talented! Even the students who "underperformed" at Banneker left to matriculate at other schools where they became big fish in a smaller academically competitive pond. All of that to say I learned how to work hard and find satisfaction in achievement. At university, I would learn the dark side of equating achievement with self-worth. The twin dark sides of anxiety and depression were things with which I battled because I began welding my self-worth to academic outcomes. If I am honest, it is still a struggle for me in my forties. Having internalized at a young age the need to achieve things (not always academic in nature), this has become a core driver that is sometimes threatening to my overall health.

Though I only came to know of "twice as hard for half as much" well after high school, I was not naïve to the forced inequality that is white patriarchal supremacy. I have the TV show *Scandal* to blame (thank?) for my critical turn against the phrase, specifically the detrimental and shame-induced consequences it can have on Black women. In the season three opener of *Scandal*, the principal character, Olivia Pope (Kerry Washington)—the owner of her own crisis PR firm—hangs her head as she listens to her father berate her for being a lump of mediocrity. In a booming, venomous tone, Eli Pope (Joe Morton)—the head of a clandestine government spy organization—unfurls his disappointment in Olivia's behavior. As his only child, he has taught her better—to strive for Black excellence. He tells her, "How many times have I told you, you must be what? Twice as good as them to get half of what they have".[15] She cannot be known as the woman having an affair with the married, white President, at least not without some kind of quid pro quo. A sexual relationship for transactional gain—say, a position as Secretary of State or Chief of Staff—would be understandable to Pope's father. But to have chosen such precarity due to the temporalities of love and desire? That, to Eli, is mediocrity incarnate, and not worth the potential professional blowback, specifically because Olivia is a Black woman.

I recall this scene both here and in my PhD thesis (Pow, 2021) because it encapsulates a false intersectional, representational dilemma for Black people, particularly the bodies and lives of Black women. I remember how Eli's abrasive behavior toward Olivia engendered praise from some of the show's Black audience because this Black patriarch was "protecting" his daughter by getting her back in line. Political power, money, and positional achievement were of undeniable value; one's internal fulfilment should be a lower priority than external achievement. A minority of fans, including me, disagreed with this version of Black excellence being something defined primarily by external validation. Olivia was made to feel ashamed for allowing herself to be vulnerable; for satisfying a curiosity and sexual need. A definition of success in which the pinnacle is rising in the ranks of domination and authority is one steeped in a colonial sense of power. I am not saying that Black people should not strive to inhabit spaces and positions denied to them for far too long because of racism or misogynoir. Instead, I implore us to consider the value systems of traditional "success", and whether or not they are aligned with who we believe ourselves to be—our whole selves. Because if we do not, externally validated "Black excellence" can leave us internally bankrupt.

It is not just fictional Black women characters whose definition of success should be broadened. Women writ large have felt the pressure to buy into patriarchally informed corporate success. Much of the "second wave" of feminism (mid-20th century) distilled the idea of gendered liberation around white, middle-class values: freedom to work outside the home earning a wage and the right to sexual autonomy. The latter is not intrinsically a claim white middle-class women hold, nor one exclusively fought for by them. But access to the capitalist world was a core tenet of a feminist movement largely run by women who saw equality as commensurate with the status of white heterosexual men. Decades later, the neoliberal idea remains that women's liberation is achieved via economic parity with men, particularly in corporatized systems.

Lean back before you "Lean In"

I was the only Black person in my Languages and Cultures of Asia master's program, and in all of my classes. But that, in and of itself, was not new to me. This wasn't my first time at the PWI rodeo. I was the only Black anthropology major at Vassar, in the three years between declaring my major and graduating around the turn of the millennium. Between University of Wisconsin (UW)-Madison and Vassar, the percentage of white people didn't differ that much, but in sheer numbers, there were a lot more white folks in Madison, and I lacked the tight-knit Black friend group that I had developed at Vassar. These white kids in my MA program were (mostly) a few years younger, and fresh off their very recent return from India after having just graduated university. They dripped with hubris and vaguely cancel-able Indian accents. It was 2003, and it had been three years since I had last been in India. I spent the last two years managing the United States Holocaust Memorial Museum's (USHMM's) *Law Enforcement and Society* ethics training program[16] for law enforcement agencies: a line of work far, far away from Indian culture. I felt rusty, unqualified to be there (despite having earned a rare fellowship to a master's program). Moreover, I wasn't sure if I could act like my fellow twenty-somethings; I had the good sense to know I did not want to model myself after their air of self-importance, or perhaps I wished for their confidence. I did not want to change myself, but I wanted to feel less disconnected from them.

Sheryl Sandberg (2013), former Chief Operating Officer of Facebook, wrote a very famous guide aimed at women who want to succeed in male-dominated workplaces entitled *Lean In: Women, Work, and the Will to Lead*. In it, Sandberg urges women to lean into those corporate environments, and to take up the charge of leadership instead of standing on the side lines as if they don't belong. Sandberg's intention here is to help women overcome the deeply ingrained imposter syndrome that makes us feel inadequate to compete. Leaning in can work if one's values are aligned with the labor environment in which they are competing. But there's a different approach I began to adopt after taking advice from a long-time mentor of mine, called leaning back. No, that mentor was not the rapper Fat Joe.

Mrs. Williams (I can't call her Lynn no matter how old I get. My grandmother would be so disappointed that I disrespected my elders) is a Black, retired leader in the Education Department of the USHMM. She has been a fixture of that institution since before it had a building. Within the first week of starting my Languages and Cultures of Asia master's program, an anxious and insecure twenty-three-year-old me called Mrs. Williams for some comfort and advice. She taught me a very valuable lesson.

"Everyone in my program seems so smart and worldly", I said. I even regaled her with stories about one white girl who hailed from Massachusetts, but inexplicably spoke English with an Indian cadence, as if her recent trip to the subcontinent had permanently altered her native accent. She had been back in the States for more than three months. Mrs. Williams, having had a laugh, got serious with me. She told me that most of my fellow students had no idea what they were doing, but that posturing was their way of contending with their own insecurities as they adjusted to a pond now containing more fish of their caliber. I, she assured me, was at least being honest with myself. Not about my inadequacy, but the general anxiety I felt about wanting to succeed in grad school. I was taking a big leap, having zero fucking idea what I would do with such a degree after completing the program. At the time, I knew of no *other* Black specialists on Indian culture(s), nor whether I wanted to stay in the museum field. What I was not, she emphasized, was unqualified or inadequate. Having worked with me in some capacity since I was sixteen, her opinion was very informed, and I trusted her intrinsically.

She told me, "Here's what I want you to do. You go into that classroom, put your big feet up on the desk and lean back in your chair. That is how comfortable they should know you are. None of your peers have a thing over your knowledge and experience". As I imagined myself in the stance she recommended, a flop sweat percolated above my brow. Could I really do that? It seemed cocky to me. As the only Black person in the program, did I need people to perceive me that way? Was this not also posturing in some way? This last question I spoke aloud.

With a perspective of me that I lacked, because I was too close to see from my attempts to lean into the stances and tones being set by my largely white university cohorts, Mrs. Williams told me the one thing I had not considered.

"All of you are in the same boat. Everyone there is pretending they know what they're doing. They don't".

Her words drove out the spell I had allowed to be cast over me. Of course, I deigned not to put my feet up on the desk, but did I metaphorically Lean Back and let my body language communicate that I belonged as if the classroom was my own living room? I sure did. The truth was I was not giving myself enough credit and was ceding too much power to those around me to set the ground rules for my experience. I come back to Mrs. Williams' advice whenever I need to regain my equilibrium and give myself a big girl pep talk.

I am not disparaging the idea of leaning in, but it is not always the best solution. Sometimes, it positions you too close for you to see the bigger picture and your place inside it. Leaning back is not about standing frozen on the sidelines, refusing to join in the game. Leaning back is about perspective and evaluation. What are the rules of the game? For whose primary gain is the game structured, and are you willing to accept those terms to play? What does winning at this game require from you and is it a sustainable offer? And importantly, who all gone be there? Who are your teammates, and do you trust them? Leaning back affords us the chance to check in with ourselves on how we want to proceed in any given environment. Just because an opportunity exists, that does not make it right for you. There may even be industry standards or traditions that you question because, when you lean back and get some perspective, they just look plain exploitative. Lean back, sometimes, when you want to decide if what is on the other side of a wall is worth the climb.

Leaning back would become a metaphorical approach for me; a piece of advice I look back on as one of the top three pieces of advice I've received in my adult life. I also find the advice to be far more of a feminist practice, especially for Black and other femmes of color. Lean Back™ is not about a literal physical stance you take, but is a mental posture to which you adapt, like a second skin, even if you're *aware* the fit is not quite right and the seams might give, forcing some of your insecurity to seep out. Lean back says, "Why not me?" My blackness has been axiomatic from early on, so being Black in an overwhelmingly white context was not a conscious consideration when I applied to Vassar or UW-Madison. By that, I mean it was not a fear. I didn't think about being Black before I landed in India. My focus was entirely about pursuing an ambition, interest, or desire. I had no grand five-to-ten-year strategic plan for my life; just the naïve self-belief that I would figure it all out. Now, with a PhD in tow, a lecturing career, and a successful personal care brand under my belt, I feel like I'm still just "figuring it out". I am so thankful to my family that, as the first to graduate college, they did not put insane pressure on me to have a career with guaranteed financial security (e.g., doctor, lawyer, engineer, accountant). They guided me in that direction, of course, but when I decided I wouldn't be going to law school and would instead major in anthropology, they did not shame me, pressure me to change, or voice disappointment. They said, "that's Kadian" and allowed me to find my way. On the other hand, if they had made me get into a lucrative field, I could have been rich ages ago. I mean …. Kidding. I'm good.

4

White supremacy is whack

The whiteness of feminism

Some of you reading this have already erected defensive shields due to this chapter's title. It is worth noting that "whiteness" is an institutional patriarchal system that promulgates racial (and other) inequalities. It is not the same as individual white people. Having said that, it is through white people that whiteness is practiced. For any movement that aims to ameliorate inequality, whiteness and the role it plays within progressive movements cannot be left unexamined. A keen blind spot in the mainstream feminist movement that underpins much of its politics is the coveting of white, hetero-patriarchal power and authority. White feminists often unreflexively define the standard of humanity and equality via the achievements and behaviors of cis-gendered white men. *Are the men getting paid X amount? Then I want that, too! Do the men have to be concerned with Y? Well, then, I should not have to be either! Women should not wear or participate in Z because men will sexualize and disrespect us!* Each one of those examples conforms to standards set by white men as the ultimate avatars of humanity, the arbiters of social possibility. It is not *feminist leadership* to uncritically uphold those standards by simply carving out our pocket inside those confines. Of course, I am not dismissing hard-won territorial gains in centuries-old fights for gender equality. Gains like voting power, reproductive rights, sexual autonomy, and the ability to be financially independent from men are all areas in which feminist activists have fought hard and made significant progress. What I am arguing is that we should redefine the terms of equality because there is more to life that what (white) men have forged in their own interests and denied to others. Their leadership is one way to exist, not necessarily the ideal. For instance, maybe we should be making more than men.

Several years ago, on a podcast called *The Read*, co-host Crissle West (2014) made a compelling argument about patriarchal disrespect toward women:

> And I just hate that people put the blame on women for men not respecting women, when men haven't respected women ever. … Don't worry about men respecting you. They're not going to goddamn respect you. Do what you want to do. Either way, whether you are on a [stripper] pole, or in the boardroom, it doesn't matter. They are still going to demean you. You're still going to be treated like you're not as good. So, do what the fuck you wanna do[17].

West, a lesbian-identified Black woman, argues that we should divest ourselves from trying to earn the respect of men because we never had it in the first place. Therefore, gaining and losing respect in the eyes of men is not within our control because it is not our game. Black women, who have historically been pushed to the margins of consideration inside politics of both race and gender, understand this need to liberate our sense of identity away from sociological rigidity, creating instead our own terms of liberation.

Young feminist AKA the big piece of chicken

Part of Black liberation is letting go of the system of patriarchy that has created binary systems to preside over so much of human existence, including race, gender, sexuality, and much more. The binary system that governs so much of our identity is deeply embedded in every fabric of our lives. Perhaps the one we most frequently encounter at an early age is the gender binary. Before I knew of the words "sexism" and "patriarchy", I was already privy to gender imbalances in my own family. Some of what I observed did not make sense to me, and adult explanations never satisfied this gender logic lacuna. *What is so special about men that God made them the heads of households? Why is it that my grandmother is the only one who cooks?* Those are just a few of the questions I formed based on gendered patterns I observed in my home.

On the topic of cooking, plates of food at the dinner table would be my first conscious lesson in patriarchy. Who made the food and to whom was it first served? The order did not comport with how understood my grandparents' roles. For as long as I can remember, my grandmother worked in the healthcare industry until she was forced to retire not long ago. She preferred night shifts over daytime ones. Such shifts allowed her to grab a nap but still run errands, clean, and cook. She kept a beautiful home, fed us, and worked full time. My grandfather was a hotel porter, sometimes doing double shifts. For at least half of their marriage in the States, Mrs. and Mr. Charles were passing in the night, sleeping in the same bed only a few nights each week.

My grandfather's jobs were the extent of his responsibilities, and most of his pay was given to my grandmother to manage. He was the stereotypical man of few words, but he was not mean or stand-offish. He was easy and kept to himself, subsisting on a diet of Clint Eastwood films and westerns. He was neither handy with tools nor a great disciplinarian, so those jobs were taken up by my grandmother. She managed every aspect of the Longfellow house and everyone in it … and brought home the bacon. But it was grandfather who received the biggest piece of chicken or whatever was being served for dinner. I loved my grandfather— or "Daddy", as we called him; even me, his grandchild, for he was my most consistent father figure. He was a slight man with tiny ankles, which one of my aunts would inherit, and for which we would forever clown her. Why did he get his food first? Why did he sit at the head of the table? Even when not present for the meal, his portion was dished up first, covered, and stored until his arrival. My grandmother would be the last to sit down to eat. I must have been eight years old when I considered this dynamic, and asked, "Why does daddy get the big piece of chicken?" (Chicken is very delicious and I'm very interested in its apportioning, OK?!) My grandmother responded, "He's the head of the house". That phrase turned over in my little, still-growing brain. But, why? My grandmother does everything! Even making sure my grandfather is included in every decision. When I'd ask for something and it was a "yes", it was conditional until my grandfather had also been asked. For his part, I think he knew my grandmother was the true authority and enquired after my grandmother's response before giving his stamp of approval.

Asking him was a ceremonial offering to patriarchy, much like the big piece of chicken. This message of patriarchy and maleness was reinforced in church sermons and in the Bible. Men were to be first in women's consideration and in life in all ways. I would fight this lesson, as it never fit comfortably into the way I made sense of the world. The intermittent role my father played in my life was not one of guidance. Ironically and sadly, it was not until I was an adult, a few years before his untimely death, that I began seeking my father's advice. As stated earlier, my grandfather's head of the family status was symbolic. I was not used to being told what to do by men. With Black women as disciplinarians at home and at school, I did not grow up looking to men as primary authority figures. The most influential men in my life were the three pastors whose churches I attended with my grandmother.

Middle- and upper-class married (mostly white) women's liberation from the domestic space and into the public economy caused ripples that are still undulating today. The rights to have women earn their own salary, build career status, and ascend corporate ladders alongside men that those progressive women pushed for in the 1960s and 1970s, manifested in the ironic 1980s hailing of the "Super Woman". A manipulative PR, feel-good moniker sold to women who entered the workforce in the "greed is good" era, the "Super Woman" was expected to be just that: superhuman. She was expected to work a full day, then perform more physical and emotional labor in the domestic space for her family (see Chapter 3's discussion). That is not equality; it is oppression covered in lip gloss. Women's wages partly went to childcare in their absence from the home. Women with high salaries could afford to outsource domestic labor to Black and Latino women, including childcare services. Black women have systematically been placed in the role of domestic care-givers for centuries, be it during enslavement, Jim Crow segregation, or the current economy of Manhattan and Park Slope nannies. As enslaved people, Black women's bodies were forced to serve the micro and macro domestic needs in America (and other colonial outposts) in order to sustain the engine of white supremacy upon which it depended. Through rape or through limited choice of enslaved partner, the children Black women delivered held economic value of involuntary labor to the white economy. They were then expected to serve as wet nurses and nannies to white children, cooks and cleaners to white families, leaving very little physical and emotional capacity for their own children, if those children were not torn from them and sold elsewhere. When slavery was all but illegal,[18] Black women were largely limited to service industry work, predominately as domestic servants in white households.

Out of the house of bondage

In 2022, an episode from the third season of the FX TV show, *Atlanta* (20162022) perfectly dramatized the existentialism of white people's simultaneous dependence upon and fear of blackness in the domestic space; even of those closest to them. In "Trini 2 de Bone",[19] an upper class, white, liberal New York couple and their young son experience a crisis after their Trinidadian nanny fails to arrive one morning. Learning that her absence is due to her sudden death impacts each of them in individual and collective ways as a family. The couple largely treat Sylvia's death as an inconvenience to the needs of their own lives. The mother is forced to contend with the practical and emotional needs of her six-year-old son in addition to those of her own; the father is forced to think about how Sylvia will be replaced, and whether he can afford the upgrade to a more "metropolitan" (read: white European or Chinese) replacement nanny. It is through their young son's mourning that Sylvia's humanity and impact is felt. Because of him, the audience is introduced to Sylvia's own family and grown up children. Their mother's emotional labor was spent toiling for another family and, in some instances, was in short supply at home. Sylvia's absence leaves emotional, spiritual, and cultural lacunae for the young boy for which she cared. That Sylvia treated the child as a six-year-old human with emotional needs that were under-fulfilled by his parents does not inspire admiration in the parents, but existential insecurity about their place in their own kid's life. Through Trinidadian music, food, and vernacular teachings, both the parents and the audience learn that Sylvia's presence lives on in the little boy. It is both surprising and discomforting to the parents. One senses that this will become an opportunity for intervention on the parents' part, steering their child away from intimate affinity with Black culture and toward a more distant tolerance.

I highlight this episode because it illustrates familiar tropes about the ways in which whiteness, irrespective of political affiliation and across historical eras, finds more value and comfort in Black labor than in Black humanity. As I watched the episode, I began to think about the Sylvia character being representative of so many Caribbean women I have known; the ones who, like my grandmother, migrated to the United States for the promise of a better life. So many of them ended up in caretaker positions like Sylvia, particularly for white people. My grandmother has been in the nursing field since her arrival in 1984. The longest period was spent as a home health aide for largely white patrons on the upper-middle-class spectrum in Montgomery County, Maryland—one of the wealthiest counties in America. I was not bitter about her absences at parent–teacher conferences or induction ceremonies (she was always at my graduations) because I knew that she was working to make my life possible, especially to compensate for my own mother's failure to do so; that the house, food, clothes that I enjoyed came from the time she and my grandfather spent catering to the white people who could afford it, perhaps so that one day I would not have to.

White denial is dangerous

White people have grown up with the notion that it is rude to talk about three things openly: money, religion, and politics. These are three things they protect the most in America. They are also the three most intertwined, consequential things in America. In some ways, those taboo topics give insight as to why white people can sometimes seem to just look past Black people: they are literally uncomfortable talking about race in a meaningful way. Race as a topic is impolite to bring up as part of someone's identity. Perhaps that is why white people think the claim "I don't see race" (racial colorblindness) is a *good* thing. But these racial blinkers can fuel inaction, leading to outcomes that have real consequences on the lives of Black people.

A few days after Donald Trump was elected president in 2016, there was much weeping and gnashing of teeth, for good reason. My wife and I were among those in mourning. There is a direct line between his election and the overturning of *Roe v. Wade* less than six years later. I worked through my anger and fear about the future the best way I know how—writing. The chapter I wrote (Pow, 2018) for *The Fire Now: Scholarship in Times of Explicit Racial Violence* examined ways to cope with the impending undoing of progressivism by looking back at examples of how Black women made it through the tumultuous Civil Rights era.[20] Many of us are familiar with the big historical moments of that past, but what about the smaller moments, the everyday struggles? Much like I did when I was a child seeking to allay my anxieties about adulthood, I looked to women who had lived through a past I would never know. The women I interviewed, now in their sixties and seventies, were young feminists in 1973 when *Roe v. Wade* passed. They celebrated that win along with white feminists at the time, knowing what the right to obtain an abortion in any state in the United States meant for their bodily autonomy and personal ambitions. I wept to know these women are still alive to see *Roe's* undoing. Their mothers, in 1973, had only been able to exercise their right to vote for just under a decade because of the Voting Rights Act of 1965 which prevents racial discrimination in voting. Those mothers' votes for Lyndon B. Johnson would lead to the first African-American on the Supreme Court, Thurgood Marshall, in 1967, who was a key part of *Roe's* passage. The mothers and grandmothers of those women are the ones who made it out of enslavement. The thirteenth amendment, the Voting Rights Act, *Roe v. Wade*—all of these are matters of civil rights directly connected to and affecting Black people. The passage of all three laws happened in as little as three generations, and in the last ten years American conservatism has been chipping away at the integrity of them.

In the immediate days following the devastating election, I wasn't yet thinking clearly. Many progressives were not. Much of the talk in the aftermath of the 2016 presidential vote was emotional, which is understandable. I witnessed a lot of people on social media (Twitter) talk about cutting out Republicans from their lives and encouraging white people to argue at the Thanksgiving dinner table with conservative family members. Singer Katy Perry admitted that her parents voted for Trump (Neophytou, 2016)— a thing that had surprised her, despite her family being white evangelical Christians her entire life. Perry became a popular target, and people urged her to throw conversational flares at the dinner table. I read these furious Twitter conversations with a numb detachment. I began cultivating strategic disengagement that year (no participating in social media debates with agitators) to protect my sanity. My heart hurt too much to sustain the energy it took to be demonstrably angry on social media. I kept my anger contained. Amid my dread, a fleeting thought hit me: I was in a liberal, progressive bubble on Twitter. I did not know most people I followed. They were distant from me, and therefore only revealing a partial story about Trump's election. None of *them* voted for Trump, but clearly a significant number of people did; ones filtered out by my Twitter algorithm. Where else could I go? Facebook. The one social media platform that I had reserved only for real-life connections. If I have never met the person or have not spoken to them since the start of the 21st century, I hit "decline" on the friend request. I do not care if it is a second cousin, or the best friend of someone I know well. *I do not know them*, and I do not collect "friends" for sport. Facebook is not a place where I cultivate new relationships; it is a place where I maintain established ones.

That early November, garden shears in hand, and logged on to carry out some pruning. Whom, among my friends' list, disappointed me the way Katy Perry's parents did her? I found two friends whose status updates blatantly indicated their Trump preference. Both were white women. Real-life voters who were counted among that fifty-five percent of white women who gave their votes to Trump.[21] Yes, it is true that, with the exception of Lyndon B. Johnson and Bill Clinton (white, southern paragons of American masculinity), the plurality of white women's votes has gone to the Republican party since 1952.[22] That this truth has existed for decades did not obliterate the hope that, perhaps, like the surge in non-white voter turnout for the first Black presidential candidate in 2008,[23] women—especially the white ones—would herald a gender-defining moment with a win for Hillary Rodham-Clinton, the first woman candidate to win any political party's nomination for United States presidential candidate. Alas, it was not to be. Their voting patterns remained consistent.

But this pattern was news to me because I was one of the many women and people of color whose hope fought the impending reality. The first friend who outed herself as a Trump voter was Sherry. Our first meeting was in India as junior year study abroad students for a Culture and Development program. In the rush of early bonding, when one tends to form connections based on superficial commonalities, we both learned we were the only two evangelical Christians in our cohort. Sherry even found herself an English-speaking church to attend in Mysore, our home base. A nice person who was committed to her faith, Sherry and I got along well enough, staying in touch intermittently. When Facebook came along a few years later, adding her as a "friend" was a no-brainer. The Sherry of 2016 delighted in Trump's win. For her, it was a return to the kind of country God intended. Such language is always code for *"Thank God the n*gger is out of office! Now back to the regular assortment of (male) whites".* I was not very surprised by this, and therefore less hurt. I hit delete with a pitiful shake of my head.

Racial statistics are most disappointing when they are realized in people we know. This was the case with Tawny, the second real friend who announced herself as a Trump supporter in a way that made it seem perfunctory. She and I attended Rockville Church of God together in my teens and early twenties. She was a true believer, but also not above selfishly bending the rules. This "bending" mostly applied to having (or doggedly pursuing) clandestine sex with single Black men in our church group. I had not kept up with her life in years, but we had been Facebook friends since I joined in the mid-2000s. It did not come as a surprise that she had married a Black man and had—according to America's narrow, binary definition of race—two Black children with said man. Her Facebook status reflected a conciliatory air: "I know we won, but we should be mindful of how disappointed the other side feels", as if it were the Super Bowl result. My expectations for Sherry were in the toilet, and we had a situational friendship. But Tawny? I was angry with her personally and politically. I had sleepovers with her. Shared secrets with her. I knew her … or thought I did. How could she, as the mother of two Black children, vote for Donald Trump to govern America? How can she look her Black husband in the face and tell him she loves him after having voted for a man who openly sees Black people as inferior and encourages the police to assault them? I had imagined the fifty-five percent of white women who voted for Trump to be partnered with white men who never deviate from the white male candidate. Or maybe with a Latino man, given that voting block's split between the two political parties. Sure, the Ginny and Clarence Thomases of the world exist, but since the two of them did not create children together, I was hoping for more from Tawny. Given her decision as a white woman who was married to a Black man and raising Black children with him, the implications had me hot.[24] I hit the unfollow button with as much impotent force as I could muster.

Some people may be wondering, what's the big deal? You ended friendships due to political preferences? Yes, Tabitha, I did. I am. I will. In the words of James Baldwin (1965): "We can disagree and still love each other unless your disagreement is rooted in my oppression, and denial of my humanity and right to exist".[25] There was no other way for me to interpret the actions of white friends who voted for Trump to be president. Each vote propped up the belief that white men are the rightful rulers of America and inherent authority figures over the rest of us. Much like misogyny, it takes a village of all kinds to maintain the system of white, hetero-patriarchal supremacy. The core foundation of such a system requires inequality for everyone else and the artificial uplift of white, heterosexual males and their attendant interests.

White people will never be the arbiters of race, nor of what is and is not racist, in the same way men will never be authorities on misogyny. Because the call is coming from inside the house. Yet white men having been getting away with deciding what is and is not racist for ages, as if they are some higher echelon human subject of a Chaka Khan song ("I'm every race, it's all in meeeeeee"). You cannot be an authority on a matter of identity for which you have no lived experience, a thing for which you are incapable of self-reflection. To paraphrase Paolo Freire (1970),[26] the oppressed know far more about their oppressor for we are forced to study them in order to create ways to outlive the obstacles they have set to barricade us in.

When many white people declared that all Trump supporters should not be labeled as racist, they said so comfortably because they think of racism as a direct, intentional act of hatred. They do not consider it in its most abundant form: deliberate oversight. That is the lack of consideration for and failure to consider Black and other people-of-color's humanity. The lack of consideration is equally dangerous. It is (usually) not active hatred that allows police officers to snuff out an unarmed Black person's life under the guise of "feeling threatened". No, that person's life was always expendable to those officers—literally worth less in America. We all grow up in such a society that inherently devalues Black humanity. In America, law enforcement, cannot be independently considered from its origins in slave patrolling, as required to enforce the Fugitive Slave Act of 1850 (Durr, 2015). The institution of policing is built on an antipathy toward Black people's freedom. Existing in our own bodies, determining the direction of our own lives was criminal. The thought is subconsciously embedded in the culture of policing. Law enforcement officers are also steeped in an organizational culture that reaffirms this to the point that it becomes axiomatic. Our lives are not considered because our humanity is not seen in equal value. The three-fifths compromise of 1787 referred to enslaved people as counting only as a fraction of a person legally, for the purpose of political representation of the slave-holding states. Extending far beyond legality, the Compromise is still deeply psychologically embedded in white peoples' collective imagination more than two centuries later.

White people owe a debt in America, one they have never paid. They continue to hold on to that two-fifths of our humanity to avoid the existential crisis that would threaten the lie of whiteness. If Black people are seen as equally human, it negates the premise of "natural" white superiority, and the very foundation American is based upon: the manufactured inferiority of Black people. Money, politics, and religion have all been used to deny full humanity to us. That manufactured, unacknowledged association between "black" and "inferior" underpins the false idealism of the colorblind approach. If you don't see my color, then there is no way you can fully see my humanity, because my race is a big part of my identity, my life. How, then, can Tawny love her husband (or he love himself if he also voted for Trump) or her children in choosing an anti-Black candidate? Maybe they are the next level of Ginny and Clarence Thomas. Interracial white supremacists with kids! As with misogyny, it takes all kinds (not only white people) to uphold white supremacy.

5
Ex-church girl

Getting saved

I was born to a girl whose sixteenth birthday passed less than three months before I arrived. My mother's younger sister, two years her junior, became pregnant at eighteen, but experienced a miscarriage. My grandmother gave birth to my mom at eighteen. All of these were unplanned pregnancies, the most consequential of which was my mother's. Teenage girls in Jamaica in the 1970s were not allowed to attend high school whilst pregnant. In a country heavily influence by protestant Christian values, my mother's condition was shameful, and set a bad example to the rest of her classmates. My mother was forced to drop out.[27] For a brief time, she did not want to carry the pregnancy to term. My grandmother, age thirty-four, had become an evangelical Christian by then. She would not allow my mother to dash weh di belly (terminate her pregnancy). Backed into a corner, my fifteen-year-old mother eventually fell in love with the idea of having a child, wishing specifically for a girl. Until she was no longer physically able, she would climb trees behind my grandmother's house and speak aloud to me *in utero* all the things she wished for my life. I think many of them were things she felt she no longer believed possible for herself now that the reality of me bloomed inside her. The little girl in me that will never die still relishes these stories. Like nostalgia-tinged reruns on TV, they are comforting, familiar, idealistic. This is not a triumphant pro-life anecdote; the rational adult in me knows my mother's story is one of girl, interrupted. I mourn for the adolescent who died and the ill-prepared adult who took her place. I see my birth as a significant altering of the course of my mother's life, one from which she never fully recovered. That's not fact, but it is my imperfect attempt at finding empathy for her decisions.

Many people defend right-to-life arguments with illogical statements such as *"But if your mother had an abortion, you wouldn't be here now! You wouldn't have won a Nobel peace prize!"* It's always some lofty, fantastical achievement conjured by the most ardent pro-pregnancy advocates. I use that term instead of "pro-life" because once the fetus leaves the womb and enters the world as a child with real needs, the energy for protecting the child's life disappears. The people who advocate to limit women's reproductive rights do not show support for economic and social policies that would help the mother or child's lives, particularly if both are non-white. To these pregnancy advocates, I say: you are correct. If my mother had ended her pregnancy, nothing I have achieved would exist. And no one would care because the memory of me would not exist. So, what is your point? Matter that never existed has no memory, no impact. That's the way the space–time continuum works. Once a thing exists, it's hard to imagine life without it. No existence, no imagination. In short, my mother could have had a better life if she ended her pregnancy and graduated high school. Or she could have met some worse fate. We'll never know. I am here and so is my mother.

The same year I watched my mother wave goodbye to me as she walked into Alderson Federal Prison Center was the same year in which I said "yes" to Jesus Christ by becoming a born-again Christian. The most important thing I remember about my 1992 conversion was how happy and proud it made my grandmother. She was a well-regarded member of our little storefront Church of God, located on a busy highway just over the DC–Prince George's County, Maryland border. Church was one of the things she looked forward to after working fifty to sixty hours a week. She protected Sundays fiercely, refusing to pick up work on that day. Having attended an evangelical church with her for years, a small part of me thought that by becoming a saved and sanctified Christian at age twelve, I could make up for the pain and debt Grandmother incurred on behalf of my mother.

I dedicated myself to Christianity, singing in the choir, becoming involved in plays, and continuing to recite Christian monologues as I had been doing for years. But now I was officially in God's army. Now my behavior was being watched more than ever: how I dressed, what I said, where I went, with whom I associated. Christianity gave me a sense of control at a rudderless time in my life. Much of the antipathy I now have toward performativity and fakeness is because I did it for ten of the most formative years of my life. The penchant to think about how my behavior and words will be perceived still affects me. I wanted so badly to be "on the right path", seen to be doing the "right thing". I did not think to question if the "thing" was right for me. But that is the exact purpose of fear and shame, which often work as a destabilizing tag team in our lives. This is especially true for those of us who are on the feminine spectrum of identity. I am being deliberate in my use of "feminine-identified" rather than "woman". Women who take on certain traits of masculinity are rewarded and seen as strong, so long as they dare not declare that they *are* men, lest they suffer consequences.[28] Men are punished for exhibiting feminine traits or showing empathy for femininity. Such behavior is seen as failing at manhood. Therefore, femininity is regarded as a problem to be regulated and displayed only within permissible contexts and through sanctioned bodies.

Christian fearmongering

I spent the first twenty years of my life simultaneously fascinated by and afraid of sex. Fascinated by its emotional effect, afraid of its physical repercussions. The latter outweighed sex's pleasure principle. Be it disease, pregnancy, or family disappointment, I feared all the things I should have. So that my fears never manifested, I avoided sex ... with a partner. In the late 1980s and 1990s, when I attended United States public schools, the HIV/AIDS crisis had hit a peak. Simultaneously, there was the national crack epidemic, war on drugs, "Just Say No" anti-drug campaign, and rising teen pregnancy rates. All of those storms converged around Black lives to impact them in ways other communities did not experience as potently. When I see the modern empathy with which state and government agencies approach Americans who have become addicted to opiates, I am at once happy to see a more empathetic, humane approach to a drug crisis, and also heartbroken because the racial disparity of the two groups suffering through drug crises makes one of them criminals and the other victims. The concrete realities of drugs and sex were connected in my elementary school, sometimes literally. I recall at least two occasions that discarded used condoms and crack needles were found on the playground in the morning. Living in "Chocolate City" was a contradiction. Washington, DC was both the epicenter of political power and a would-be-state with no voting power in Congress government. The then "murder capital" of the USA was also a hotspot for HIV/AIDS, crack-cocaine, and teen pregnancies.[29] With all of these disastrous circumstances, no wonder it was difficult for me to conceive of sex in life-affirming ways. Its association with death and decay was hard to escape. My family's values added personal and spiritual layers of pressure that reinforced the political and social messages I absorbed from the news and in school.

By the age of nine, I was reciting back to my Physical Education & Health teacher the ways in which one could and could not become HIV-positive. She drilled into our little brains the facts as we knew them back then. Yes, at nine years old I knew HIV was contracted through exchange of bodily fluids and that infection was not limited to homosexual men. The knowledge was important. But the fear of this disease was so stigmatized through its association with sex and drugs, it was enough to regulate me away from wanting sex with another human for a very long time. Looking back, the strict moral imperative against pre-marital sex in Christianity calcified fears that I already harbored. At the same time, the societal fears that permeated messages in schools and media I consumed were a direct influence of the evangelical groups like Jerry Falwell's "Moral Majority" and their lobbying of the Regan and Bush Sr's administrations. White evangelical supremacist Christianity and its punitive agenda was at the heart of it all. They got me. Perhaps becoming an official

Christian would ensure that I did not end up like my mom, a young woman seduced by the quixotic life of the drug trade and eventually imprisoned.

Dazed and confused

My participation in church activities was choppy during my first two years at Vassar College. By the end of my time there, I was transitioning away from Christianity and all of organized religion. A nearly six-hour drive from Washington DC, the depressed economy of Poughkeepsie, New York was still reeling from the IBM lay-offs in the late 1980s. Vassar was gated, closed off literally and symbolically. As a result, it did not have the best "town–gown" relations. The mostly working-class residents did not have great affinity for the college, which was the least depressing place in Poughkeepsie when I arrived in 1997. For their part, the students did not venture too much beyond the few local businesses bordering the campus. I knew no one in the town. That is, until a few weeks after I settled into college life. That was when Grandmother asked if I had found a church to attend. The guilt washed over me when I answered. I had not even thought about it, though I had continued to pray and read the Bible semi-frequently. My grandmother took care of this lack in my life by introducing me to Peggy. She was the daughter of a man my grandmother cared for at the time. Peggy grew close with my grandmother on visits down to Maryland to check up on her father's health, which my grandmother oversaw as his home health aide. In my freshman year Peggy, would occasionally pick me up, take me to lunch, drive me around for my errands, and so on. The emissary grandmother deployed to ensure my continued church attendance, Peggy, one day mentioned that my grandmother lamented that I had no luck finding a church. Gulp. Peggy, a former International Business Machine (IBM) executive, knew a lady who could fix that for me: a Jamaican lady who lived nearby attended church with mostly Jamaicans. Perhaps I would like that? Peggy would call her. It was set.

Two Sunday mornings later, I waited on the steps of Strong dormitory for Sister Valerie to arrive. Instead, Brother Robinson pulled up in an early 1990s burgundy Honda Civic.[30] I peered curiously at the car because I expected to see someone else. I did not know this man, but he knew my name, knew Sister Valerie, and knew that I was to be taken to Hope of the Redeemer Church of God.[31] I was satisfied with his answers and got in the car. You see, he passed close to Vassar College, and it made sense that he be the one to pick me up, he said.

I was nearly thirty before I learned to yield to my instincts, especially the unease bubbling up in my nervous system, my body's language for "get out". I felt that feeling before when assessing people, places, and propositions, and did not always heed it. That day I climbed into the car and wished I would have trusted myself more. I look back at being in that confined space with Mr. Robinson, the tension present in my body every time I sat next to him. I assuaged myself each time by remembering his moral duty as a Christian. Until that point he had not advanced himself on me, but something inside me, a premonition, knew that he would eventually do so. Mr. Robinson found opportunities to talk in sexual ways, innuendos, but was careful never to directly implicate me. Still, it made me uncomfortable. I did not like the way he lingered as he hugged me goodbye each Sunday afternoon when he drove me back to campus, the way he seemed to sneak glances at me when he thought I wasn't looking. It got to the point where I had to talk myself into going to church because my body revolted, dread dropping like a stone and weighing down my Saturday night to the point where I could not sleep peacefully. My anxiety was so great that, without fail, I would need the toilet when I got back to my dorm room. *What was wrong with me? Is this in your head? No one's done anything to you.* My inner voice would talk me off the ledge of paranoia, wanting to be wrong about Mr. Robinson. This isn't like Reverend Thornton, who always found ways to have a part of his body touch a part of your adolescent one. Not like Uncle Herbert, who tried, unsuccessfully, to penetrate you at age eight in the basement. Nothing has happened to you this time, I told myself.

One early Sunday morning, I called Mr. Robinson to say I would not be going to church. I had two exams the next day, I lied. I did not feel great about the lie, but I did feel good not being in church. The next Sunday, refreshed, I headed back to church, trying to put it all behind me. On the way back to my dorm, the proverbial "other shoe" dropped after two anxiety-riddled months of these car trips. Mr. Robinson reached across me to open my door, brushing his hand across my left breast! It was no accident. He did not acknowledge what he did, but his guilt lingered in the silence between us. I was right, after all, and it brought me no solace, only disquiet. My brain and body registered this shock, but a small part of me, in disbelief, wanted to extend the benefit of the doubt to him. It would have been easier to pretend it was an innocent mistake. But I could not stomach that version of events. I got out of the car without accusation, thanking him for the ride without looking back. I knew it would be the last time I would see that man or go to that church. In fact, I didn't bother looking for another church in Poughkeepsie. My mind and my body became closed off to the prospect. Fellowship with the Bible study group I later found on campus would have to suffice.

Selling Jesus in the 'hood

Amy and Jodie, from Colorado and Ohio, respectively, ran a small Bible study group during my freshman year. This was my second attempt at joining a Bible study group at an educational institution. My junior year at Banneker, I joined a newly formed group which was headed by a freshman named Taija. If her Bible wasn't in her backpack, it was in her locker. She almost always wore pants, the latest Jordans on her feet, and a slicked-back ponytail with a perfect side part. If I had gaydar back then, I might have made assumptions. She was pretty—clear, smooth, caramel skin, and a narrow but long nose that had a prominent beauty mark. Taija spoke with the stereotypical cadence of a Black pastor cum high school football coach on the TV show *Friday Night Lights*.

For Taija, fellowship meant taking the word of God directly into the neighboring community around our school. Her intrepid outlook made sense, but I had developed an aversion to proselytizing that had less to do with Christianity and more to do with the aversion to direct sales that I developed years before. Though a significant charge for Christians, "winning souls for Christ" reminded me too much of elementary school, where I was made to approach strangers to sell confections, cheese logs, petit fours, and wrapping paper from a catalog in exchange for a prize that was worth five percent of the value I sold. We were told that selling from these catalogs was an important fundraising activity for our public school. Why does a nine-year-old have to go knock on doors to fund raise for school activities? Could a bake sale not suffice? In wealthier counties, the school system was either adequately funded, or parents could afford to write checks for activities, or put on fundraising events. I developed a potent fear of rejection during those elementary school years when I was made to be a salesperson. Having spent several years in retail as an adult, I eventually learned the necessity to project confidence in yourself and the product you are selling, otherwise the prospective customer will sniff out the insincerity and reject your offer. Proselytizing is a form of sales. You must *convert* the customer to close the sale. Jesus is the lifestyle product you are trying to sell. In America, there is no separation between church and capitalism, only coveted tax breaks. In some ways, churches are structured like corporations, replete with regional managers and even franchising models. They have to keep money from their parishioners (customers) circulating in order to keep their business model alive, but have significantly less government oversight than corporations. Rod Morrow, co-host of one of my favorite podcasts, *The Black Guy Who Tips*, has spoken often about what an irresistible scam starting a church is. Any conman worth their salt can develop the character of a pastor and fleece their faithful flock of their cash. The grift is so tempting because faith-based institutions in America are the least likely to be scrutinized and receive undue grace. In fact, being a "religious worker" is a legitimate path toward an American residency visa (Green Card), though the language for this path is heavily skewed toward interpreting "religious" as Christian.[32] Jesus is a product in infinite supply, and the demand is easy to create. Where I believed as a teenager that my Christian beliefs were personal, for most leaders of Christian institutions, it's business. Big business.

By age sixteen, I had been familiar with "the product", Jesus, for several years. I should have been confident in its benefits, but instead I kept my belief in Christ as a mostly personal way to govern myself and justify my fears. Still, I was overcome by anxiety the Friday afternoon Taija announced our Bible study session was being replaced by a field trip along Georgia Avenue to introduce people to God's word. First, Taija would lead by example while the rest of us watched how it was done. The rest of us would go off in pairs and do the same as her. I will never forget listening in as she spoke to a handsome man with a beard and dark skin outside a corner store. He was flanked by two other guys. They looked like they had recently played basketball. One of the men, Mr. Handsome, became the de facto spokesperson for his group. He and Taija were in a tete-a-tete as we all watched them volley. For everything Taija said about the Bible and God's deliverance, Handsome had a calm, reasoned rejoinder. I found myself ready to be de-converted by him. It was not physical attraction to him that drove this. His sincerity spoke to deeply held questions I had been too afraid to ask for fear of being labeled a heretic. Why does God allow so much suffering to happen under his watch? Where was God in the last ten years as Mr. Handsome watched his community deteriorate? Why do people who profess Jesus' name commit so much evil in this world? Taija was never without a response, but she did not walk away from the discussion with Handsome as a triumphant spokeswoman for Jesus. The prospective customer was too secure in his life and experiences to be sold on Jesus. Thinking back, what was Taija—a fourteen-year-old girl—going to tell that nearly thirty-year-old man about living life? Suffice it to say, when we were dispersed into proselytizing pairs, I let my Bible study partner take the lead as my doubt surged ahead of my passion for Christianity.

I tucked away those doubts by the time I reached Vassar. The incident with Mr. Robinson had put me off church, but not off Christianity and its potential to make new friends on campus. Amy and Jodie's Bible study was more laid-back than Taija's. White girls from Colorado and Oregon, respectively, everything about their leadership was high energy, low pressure—or the appearance of it. I felt secure enough about the group to invite Margaux, my Haitian Catholic friend from Brooklyn, only because I knew she was curious about the evangelical branch of Christianity. I had spent a weekend at her house over Easter and attended Mass with her. It was my first time at a Catholic service. Boy, was it profoundly boring. Too much ceremony, standing and sitting, with little joy and energy to give it some *jujh*. Catholicism contrasted sharply with the singing and effusive displays of worship I was used to in evangelical churches. When Margaux later inquired about my Bible study group, I invited her to attend with me and see for herself. After several more sessions, she was ready to formally accept Jesus into her life. I hoped God would give me credit for this soul.

Margaux was serious about her turn to evangelical Christianity. As time passed, we were headed in opposite directions on the Christian journey. By senior year, when I returned from a semester abroad in India, I started letting go of a lot of the control I'd been indoctrinated to have over my body, mind, and behavior.

Margaux, on the other hand, remained on campus her entire junior year. While I was gone, she became even tighter friends with Amy and Jodie, strengthening both her Christian faith and their fellowship. Mine, on the other hand, had dissipated.

I think the death knell of my friendship with Margaux sounded when, in senior year, I chose to spend spring break with my first real boyfriend, Jordan, in lieu of going with my friends (including Margaux) to the United States Virgin Islands. When, weeks later, I announced that I was no longer a virgin, the rift between us began. Margaux had already sensed I was "backsliding" away from God. My announcement merely confirmed her suspicions. Virginity (for women) was important in the church, and I had brazenly announced that I no longer believed in that importance. By this point, Margaux was more heavily engaged with the Christian campus group than I ever was, rising to co-leadership alongside Jodie and Amy. Meanwhile, our non-Christian friend group, established since freshman year, often did things without Margaux because she was busy with the Christians. I felt her pulling away but was unsure of what to do. Once we graduated, she stopped speaking to me altogether. She did, however, continue speaking to our mutual friends, none of whom were, or had ever, identified as Christian. The withdrawal of her friendship hurt me, pricked at my easily ruptured sense of shame. But it was her right to take away her friendship. She never explained it to me or anyone else in the group, but I managed to make sense of it. I, as the person who introduced her to the Lord, was now a disappointment who had turned her back on Him. I became a dangerous influence, a backslider (like my pregnant teenage mother represented for other girls at her own school). Our other friends were who they had always been. *I* was the one who had changed.

Sex and the Christian girl

It was the sex that did it for Margaux; the sex that I was having and enjoying. More than any other sin, evangelical Christians (and Mormons) are obsessed with consenting bodies engaged in the "sin" of sex outside the regulated confines of monogamous marriage between opposite sexed couples (unless you are a member of the Fundamentalist Latter-Day Saints (FDLS)) that could result in a child. Sex, as a life-affirming act between people, is only celebrated in Christian circles because of its potential to yield "fruit", as in "be fruitful and multiply". Of course, Christians enjoy sex for sex's sake, but celebrating it within the confines of marriage allows them to wield moral superiority over the rest of us. They are doing it the "right" way. According to them.

As I write this, the Supreme Court of the United States (SCOTUS) has officially trampled over *Roe v. Wade*, rescinding federal protection of the right to terminate a pregnancy, and leaving that right up to the individual states. At least one-third of these have already enacted laws to curb or eliminate women's bodily autonomy. This 2022 decimation of legal precedent was something Christians felt was long overdue, having worked to overturn *Roe* since its passage in 1973. What an unmitigated dedication to discrimination.

Extreme Christians are not pro-life; they are pro-punishment. Punishing disobedience is tantamount to an orgasm for them. The Puritan and Calvinist roots of the early settlers run deep in America's psyche, particularly the Christian and Christian-adjacent sects (looking at you Mormons and FLDS). An unmarried pregnant woman or teen must give birth because the pregnancy, and the resulting child, are the evidence of disobedience. A woman engaging in sex for her own pleasure should face consequences for her unsanctioned lust. Stay in your lane or else! The child resulting from the pregnancy is the living manifestation of the woman's punishment for sexual autonomy. Men's participation in the sex act is not acknowledged or punished. This is how we know denying reproductive care is specifically about maintaining patriarchal order, for which limiting women's independence is necessary. That is the only thing that makes sense to me when I think about the discrepancy between the performative zealotry for zygotes and fetuses many Christians proclaim and the complete disregard for funding early childhood programs, public education, non-religious adoption, or even legislating maternity and paternity leave. It is not, nor has the purported "pro-life" stance ever been, about the child's life or wellbeing, but about restricting women's autonomy and agency.[33] They use their beliefs to protect themselves and rule over the lives of non-believers in a way that is reminiscent of the Dark Ages in Europe. I don't think Margaux was conscious of any of the above when she became disappointed that I was sexually active. And I realize much of what I have written in this section is a very ungenerous take, but on this matter, I am bereft of generosity.

By the time I was ready to attend graduate school, I was decidedly no longer a Christian.

6

Sex and the Black Christian girl

Puberty exposed

I approached first-time sexual intercourse more strategically than romantically. It was my senior year in college, and I was twenty-one. I did not feel rushed by my peers or impending graduation to relinquish my identity as "virgin". One day, my body was ready to have sexual intercourse with a partner. In fact, for the majority of my life, and up until the year before, I planned for my first sexual experience to be with my husband on our wedding night. Such was the expectation for a born-again Christian girl, like me, who had given her life to Christ at the age of twelve. But my mind and body converged around the idea of copulation well ahead of any potential husband I would meet. This readiness coincided with the crisis of faith I began experiencing the previous year whilst in India. The more I unabashedly questioned the rigid boundaries of my faith, the more relaxed and open my body became. I had imagined that being on top of a man would begin in my late twenties, giving my husband and me a couple of years of unfettered enjoyment before having children. Oh, to be young and naïve.

I laugh now because, as I write this, more than twenty years after my first sexual encounter, I am child-free by choice and married to a woman. I could not have foreseen this trajectory for my life. Now deeply satisfied with life's curveball, I think about the many choices I have made—as a woman who is Black and queer—that have brought me along this path and not the one my under-developed teenage mind myopically conceived. I have been curious about and fascinated with sex since the age of five. That is the age at which I was accidentally exposed to explicit pornography. Porn is its own specific category of sexual fantasy and not a total reflection of sex, but at the age of five, my brain could not comprehend this. I was too overwhelmed and stunned by its sensorial effect. The noises coming from the TV, the flashes of skin and hair on the screen, that *was* sex to me; the nasty thing that adults did with each other. This exposure is every parent's nightmare scenario for their child; the corrupting trauma origin story that goes on to negatively skew the child's expectations of and interactions with the opposite sex (most parents have heterosexual expectations for their children, even latently so). It was not my trauma or villain origin story. It was a memory I held secretly for a long time; one I sometimes held out for distant examination, and at other times chastised myself about, feeling a deep sense of shame when I could not live up to the moral tenets of Christianity.

I can only recall pieces of what happened the day sex was made visible for me. I was living with my mother and her paternal aunt in Kingston, Jamaica. My mother's parents and siblings had left for America, and we would not join them until I was nearly seven. With me in tow, my mother trudged across the street to her friend's house. I remember standing on the friend's porch, hearing strange noises coming from the other side of the door. My mother was used to walking into her friend's house, unannounced, and this time was no different. Except, this time, she entered, loudly complaining. There, in the living room, was her friend's brother, on his day off from the police force, watching a "blue" video.

"Ah you bring yuh pickney to mi house".

"Miggle a day and you in ya bein nasty. Why yuh nuh go watch in a yuh room?"

"Is in ya suh the TV and VCR deh. Chuh raatid!"

These are not exact quotes, but this was the tenor of the argument, in Jamaican patois. The brother was angry to have his relaxation time interrupted by our unannounced visit. My mother was disgusted that he would be "relaxing" in the family room instead of doing so in his own room, in private. Their passionate fault-finding allowed me time to fix my eyes on the screen for what could not have been more than a minute or two. I was too shocked and mesmerized by what I had seen to care anything about their argument. Cheap red, stretched lace lingerie, brown skin, glossy black hair full of large, flouncy 1980s curls, legs splayed open, hairy vulva on show, a penis in her mouth: those are the things I remembered before I was yanked out of the house. Disgusted was not something I felt that day. Curious and alert? Yes. I played the scenes over and over in my mind, recognizing that it did something to my body that I could not explain at the time, but found exciting in a way I knew was bad. This is because, afterward, my mother apologized to me for what I had seen. Videos like that are for nasty men, she told me. From that I learned that not only were the things happening in that video clearly not for children, but they were also not for adult women either, only men. The "nasty" kind.

Sex, masturbation, and the good girl

Whether in the Caribbean or the United States, diasporic Black culture employs the word "nasty" in multiple contexts to mean undesirable or improper behavior.[34] That may have been my first lesson in shame, and it would be something I internalized as I grew older and felt sexual desire blossoming in my body. By age eleven, when I discovered there was power and pleasure in touching myself, I hid this knowledge. I hid the masturbatory behavior. I learned to be quiet. I learned to rewind family members' "nasty" video tapes to the precise points at which they had left them. Most of all, I learned how to beg for God's forgiveness after each orgasm, a practice I continued until I took my life back from religion in my early twenties.

The thing about feeling pleasure is it is powerful and consuming. Too pre-occupied with heady sensations, the mind has no room to feel fear or shame in the moment. Those things come after climax, like clockwork, in what is called *post-coital tristesse*. An amalgamation of Latin (*post-coital* meaning after sex) and French (*tristesse* meaning sadness), its literal meaning is post-sex sadness. It describes the anxiety or worry that one is flooded with after orgasm. This was the case for me. I would feel amazing and that was quickly replaced by the thought of God's disappointment in me because I knew I should not have been touching myself. I would sometimes cry, begging for forgiveness. Each time I really wanted to mean it. The bright side was that the soporific effect of the melatonin that follows the post-orgasmic release of oxytocin meant that the bad feelings were always fleeting, displaced by sleep. Until the next time. In this way, girls learn to find shame in our bodies before some of us even begin menstruating, another thing we are encouraged to see as deficient.

Ironically, this pleasure–shame cycle was the lesser of two evils for me. The greater evil was sexual activity with boys. That, I would not risk. When I began menstruating at the age of twelve, I told my born-again Christian grandmother, who, by that point, had already been my primary parent for years. I can still vividly recall our bathroom at the time, where the conversation took place. We had a wicker laundry hamper with a thick wooden lid. The whole thing was covered in azure blue paint. She sat me down on top of that hamper and told me, "this means you don't let boys touch you". I nodded my head, assuring her that I understood the message and the implications. Though it occurred to me, I probably would have been slapped had I asked, "wait, was it OK for boys to touch me *before* this?"

My mother was several months shy of turning sixteen when she became pregnant with me. Her younger sister, my aunt, also became pregnant as a teenager, but miscarried. My mother's youngest sister (nineteen years her junior) became a mother at the age of sixteen. My elder sister welcomed my niece at nineteen. Even my grandmother became pregnant with my mother when she was just eighteen. It was now up to me to break the cycle of pregnancy in the family, an assignment I gave to myself. After all, my grandparents had not worked hard to bring my mother and me to Washington, DC only for me to do something I could have stayed in Jamaica to do. No, I was brought to the United States to go farther than anyone else in my family had gone by that point in 1991. Despite the conversation by the blue clothes hamper, my grandmother did not repeatedly give me warnings about keeping my legs closed. She said what she said, and I received the message. I had resolved to escape the fate of the very fertile women in my family by having no romantic connections with boys during my teenage years. I could not take the chance. I can acknowledge now that I internalized this pressure much more than any that was externally placed upon me by any family member. They find grace for me when I cannot locate it in myself.

This avoidance of sex had several consequences, ranging from empowering to obfuscating. Because I had already learned how to pleasure myself before I started menstruating, I knew that I did not need anyone else to provide that for me. Unlike boys, who are actively encouraged to seek out the bodies of teenage girls and women as part of their ritualistic crossing over into manhood, girls are not taught that our adolescent identities are predicated upon relationships with boys. If we are virginal, we are still considered women. In fact, in many religious circles, the virginity of a girl is a highly prized feminine trait. Whilst not actively discouraged from relationships with boys, girls are encouraged to be wary of their hyperactive, sex-seeking adolescent hormones because they endanger our lives. I was also clinically obese by the age of thirteen, so I am certain that fact helped make me less of an attractive prospect to teen boys. In any case, I made virginity a mission of my teen years, instead devoting my energies to friends, church, and becoming a top prospect for universities. I would be the first in my family to graduate from university. I wanted to achieve this not just for my own ego, but as a "win" for the family. I wanted the younger kids coming after me to see that at least one of us had done it, which meant they could, too. Though she is my aunt, my mother's youngest sister, Sherene, is like a sister. She's proven to be a fantastic and attentive mom to all her children. Though Sherene did not attend college, the daughter she had at sixteen, Dejah, is a member of the historically Black Delta Sorority and graduated with a bachelor's degree in 2021. Her younger sister, Saebrin, is a sophomore at a university in Virginia.

Teen pregnancy: a fate worse than death

Romantically recoiling from boys left room for academic focus and intense friendship-building. But the lack of sexual interaction with boys had a muddling effect on my sexual identity. I did not use that time to explore my own sexual attractions. Was I queer back then? It is hard to say. I don't recall being physically attracted to the bodies of women at that time. Even when consuming "nasty" videos, male genitalia was a requirement for me to feel stimulation. Of course, with the way desire and sexual attraction functions, this means very little. Our fantasies do not strictly adhere to our sexual realities. Fantasy is a space for play, exploring variety, and safely flirting with danger. What we allow ourselves to imagine does not necessarily have real bearing on reality unless we choose it to do so.[35] In fantasy, we can make ourselves powerful by casting ourselves as the conductor of the train, determining its destination, whereas we sometimes feel like passengers in reality just along for the ride. My fantasy world gave me an emotional harbor during adolescence, where I could dock my *S.S. Desire* without judgment. But I was never completely free in my imagination because I actively shunned thoughts of queer sex. Imagining that kind of sex felt as if it would double the sense of shame I felt afterwards; double the amount of forgiveness I would have to seek from Jesus after climaxing. This speaks to the greater obfuscating cloud hanging over my teen years: Christianity. The fear of being queer came only second to my fear of becoming pregnant.

Multiple factors coalesced to make me deathly allergic to becoming a pregnant teen. In my mind, having a mother, two aunts, and a grandmother who were pregnant teens made me very susceptible to the same fate. My clan was extremely fertile, I reasoned. This thought plagued me for my entire sexual career with men, despite being a dedicated taker of birth control pills. But as a teenager, I resigned myself to the safer option of abstinence. In fact, to avoid any form of sexual pressure from boys, I discarded the idea of teenage love. I did not want a boyfriend. Boys + sex = inevitable baby and life ruination. No, thank you.

A vague understanding of the id, super id, and ego was the extent of my knowledge of psychology in high school. I did not understand the subconscious brain with any sophistication (I still don't). After several bouts of cognitive behavioral therapy (CBT) since age nineteen, looking back, I can see that becoming a born-again Christian who was expected to wait until marriage to have sex gave me an excuse to avoid boys and the pregnancy laser beam tucked away in their pants. I was determined it would never be pointed in my direction. I also felt secure in the fact that I was not one of the highly desirable girls. Even with some acne,

I was a pretty girl. But I was also quite fat in an era when body positivity discourse was not mainstream. I was not positive about my body. After my mother went to prison, and my eighth-grade plans (I was set to change schools and move in with her) were thrown into disarray, I became clinically obese by the time I was thirteen. At two hundred and thirty pounds in a 5'7" frame, I was sure no one wanted me anyway. For that I was glad. I felt secure in being liked among girls, but not the primary choice of any boy. Whilst Black men are the most likely to find curvy and "thick" body types sexy, I am speaking of teenage boys. They are less secure about their desires because they care very much what their fellow adolescent boys think. They are trying to find their masculinity and this is a most fragile period for it. Their choice of girls tended to weigh at least fortyfifty pounds less than me.

Overweight-Christian-desperately-dodging-a-fate-worse-than-death (pregnancy) was the majority of my teenage identity. As an evangelical Christian, abortion was out of the question, so sex needed to be avoided at all cost to prevent pregnancy in the first place. I was rigid about boys touching my body, but I was very practiced at touching myself. I distinctly remember that I was eleven years old when I discovered my clitoris and how it shivered my timbers when I touched it a certain way. It was the summer of 1990 and I was at my mother's apartment in Greenbelt, Maryland. Bored of seeing the same dozen music videos on "The Box" as I lay under a blanket with the frigid air conditioner blasting down on me, my hands began wandering south. Alone in the living room, my legs were open as I absentmindedly fondled myself out of boredom. That's when I discovered that feeling. Because I happened upon it by accident, not strategy, I kept trying to repeat the feeling. My mother came out of her room whilst I was investigating this, and said, "is whah yuh a do?" I think she knew, but I answered, "nothing" and straightened up. We left it there. I had a room to myself by this age, at my grandmother's house. I eventually figured out what to do to make myself orgasm, and it felt like I had unlocked a very critical part of the game of life.

The idea and the fantasies of sex were not the problem for me; the potential reality was. I did not have family members explain sex in ways that were not bound up in fear. To me it was portrayed as impermissible, bad, wrong, though all the adults engaged in it. As a Christian, my own sense of bodily pleasure was in deep conflict with what was expected by my faith. I had been taught that not only was fornication a sin, but so too was watching pornography and masturbation—separately and together. I never managed to give up either one, even in the post-orgasmic disgust with myself when I pleaded with Jesus for forgiveness. I would promise not to do it again if he could just forgive this one last instance. The last instance never came, though I always did. Even after leaving the church behind and renouncing my born-again status in my early twenties, it would take me until age twenty-five to finally rid myself of lingering feelings of guilt and shame around self-pleasure. I thought of sex and dreamed up sexual scenarios between imaginary people often. It's a wonder I was so intrigued by sex when, in the early 1990s, health teachers went out of their way to portray sex as fearsome and gross, or simply as anodyne biology. My inappropriately young introduction to pornography piqued my interests about what naked adults do with their bodies. In a way, I prefer that introduction to sex than the one I received in health class; the one in which we were made to watch hours of footage showing the diseased consequences resulting from sex with the "wrong kinds" of people. That approach was not born of concern for sexual health. As mentioned earlier, the socio-political climate had much to do with this puritan-based way of learning about sex, but it is also true that the intent was to make sex seem dangerous and potentially fatal in its wounding. Though I do not recommend that children are exposed in the way I was, I am glad I saw the pleasure first, though I later learned how manipulative the pornography industry is. Pleasure in our bodies is so powerful, no wonder we are made to fear it first.

Sex as a disease

I can recall one of the most embarrassing moments of my early teens when I tried to get revenge on a boy, Dewayne, in my seventh-grade class. He constantly made fun of my weight, though he was also clinically obese. One day, when boarding the yellow school bus that was to take us back to our class after an outing at the Sumner School, I tripped up the stairs. In front of everyone Dewayne yelled, "It's your world big girl; you fall, you take us all!" Laughter roared and I seethed. Where did this big motherfucker get off? Of course, I now understand that women are held to higher standards under gendered regimes of beauty and bodily attraction. This difference is exemplified on every profile picture of a plain-looking man who deigns to jealously comment on the social media posts of women who would never even bat a fake eyelash at him. And the sentiment fuels the toxic entitlement and self-victimization of those who call themselves involuntarily celibate (InCels). Men resent the very standards they are responsible for setting and upholding under patriarchy when those standards are made to work against them. This is why those who lack the skills (or are afraid) to engage with women as their fellow human beings hate women who embrace their agency and bodily autonomy: because if we get to choose in the marketplace of men, according to narrow patriarchal rules that denote men as providers of financial and physical security, some men lose out. But it is women who are blamed, called "shallow b*tches", for abiding by the system that men created, and from which many of them benefit.

I bided my time with Dewayne. I let him wait days before I did something petty (but now read as homophobic at worse, problematic at best). I drew a diseased penis on a piece of blue construction paper, replete with an unsightly drip extending from the tip. I managed to tape it to the back of his sweatshirt without him being aware. It lasted all of twenty minutes, but oh how it tickled me and my friends. One of Dewayne's buddies noticed the symbolic signage on his back and told him about it. It did not take long for someone to snitch on me. Dewayne promptly told Mrs. Middleton, our principal. I wondered if it was the drip that took it over the top or if he was also a bit homophobic, and decided this was to be escalated beyond a tete-a-tete between us. Mrs. Middleton was disappointed in me because I was "a good girl". Her soft spot for me saved me from detention, but the punishment she meted out resulted in a far worse shame. I was to take the penis cut-out home, have my parents sign it, and return it to Mrs. Middleton the next day. I never craved a month's detentions as much as I did then. When I told my grandmother what I had done and showed her what she needed to sign, she was hot with anger! She said, "Is this what you're in class thinking about all day?" forcefully shoving the periwinkle penis toward my face. That she used a formal American accent to relay her displeasure chilled me further. I did not want to say anything clever, so I just bowed my head, dutifully mirroring her disappointment. She signed it and made my grandfather sign it, too. I was out of the prank game after that.

When I think about the diseased, construction-paper penis that I pinned to Dewayne's back, it exemplifies how much the idea of shame was commensurate with sexual education. In fact, we were not learning about sexual education at all, but a combination of human reproductive education as one of the consequences of sex, the other outcome being contracting a sexual disease. This was the 1990s, an era of high teen pregnancy and fearmongering about HIV/AIDS and homophobia were tentpoles of our "sexual" education. Well before the George W. Bush administration promoted abstinence as the preferred form of sex ed in the 2000s, the fearmongering in the 1990s around sexual engagement was already designed to inspire abstinence. Christian denial and Puritan lust for sexual shame is embedded in the cultural fabric of America; so deeply ingrained that it has become naturalized as "the way it is", which is a fallacy. These religio-cultural drivers are why we are more comfortable pushing to the forefront disease, pregnancy, medical terminology, and violence as the main components of sexual education that we teach children.

My exposure to pornography at an early age is, unfortunately, much more common these days for young people, as most people carry the internet in their pockets, where information is abundant but knowledge is lacking. In this environment, teens can grasp the mechanics and aesthetics of sex information well before any school curricula choose to divulge or foolishly censor them. What young people need help comprehending is the human connection and types of relationships that are the foundation of all things sexual. That includes our relationships with our imagined selves and real, changing bodies. We need emotional intelligence and relationship-building education in schools.

Attractive versus attraction

As girls grow up, we learn how to make ourselves attractive to boys, to men. The messages we received are both subliminal (clothing choices, posture) and direct (being told to be pretty, look nice). Boys grow expecting that we will present ourselves for their delight and consumption; that it is within their purview to objectively deign us worthy of their sexual attention. As girls, we learn how to perform sexual attractiveness before we understand ourselves as sexual beings and what it feels like to be sexually attracted to someone else. We learn the mechanics of sexual intercourse and its attendant consequences well before we learn what it feels like to *want to have* intercourse with another person, or with ourselves.

I knew I was attractive to people before I understood what it felt like to feel attracted to someone. Knowledge of my own attractiveness stemmed primarily from my family members, who plied me with unsolicited feedback from an early age. Jamaicans are brutally honest to a fault. Despite being overweight for the majority of my first two decades, my portliness was not equated with my beauty and—later—attractiveness; not in

Black communities—both Jamaican and American. The same extended family who would called me "big eeehn" were the same ones who called me "pretty gyal". Unfortunately, some adult Black men were not shy or ashamed to be attracted to a teenage girl, letting me know as early as twelve years old. I had only just started getting breasts, which would never amount to much. There is one catcall incident that is forever seared into my brain, enabling me to this day to quote it. I was fourteen, walking to the People's Drug Store (now CVS)—to get what, I can't remember. But Earl had to let me know what was on his mind, so much so he made it a couplet:

> Hey, girl, my name is Earl
> and I wanna be your squirrel!

He yelled this at me from across the street, in front of the pink-colored brick of the neighborhood flower shop. I was too stunned to say anything back. I continued on my way. Washington, DC has got to be one of the top cities for this kind of street harassment, which is what I know it to be now as an adult. As a fourteen-year-old, I thought that this was just how men were, and that I should not expect different from them. It was not until the 2010s, when the discourse around street harassment became more openly critical on social media, that I began to understand how damaging and dangerous these forms of harassment can be; how much they can linger in one's psyche, spreading shame for simply publicly existing in a female body. I would eventually learn how to navigate this unwanted attention, as well as understand that the things these men yelled at me from their cars, or on the streets, ultimately had nothing to do with me. The catcalls I received on the streets of Washington, DC taught me that merely existing in this body, with this face (DNA I did not write), was all it took for heterosexual men to feel entitled to comment on my body, including requesting that I smile. Their feelings have nothing to do with who I am, which consists of more than the fluctuating body in which I live.

As a church-going teenager, I hung out with a multicultural group, nearly half of whom had Jamaican parents like myself. Filipinos and white Americans rounded out that group. Because we spent so much time together, bound by the same biblical rules, under the same watchful glare, we were in the same predicament: brimming with adolescent sexual hormones that were gated by the limitations of our faith. Crushes developed within the group, some of which turned into secret relationships never to be spoken of outside the circle.

I developed a crush on a boy within my church circle: a white boy named Teddy. I would not be shocked to be told he grew up to be a tacit Trump supporter; the kind who does not brag, but still lends approval at the ballot box. I'm not exactly going out on a limb to say that about most heterosexual white Christian men. But back when I knew very little of his politics and was a conservative myself, my crush on Teddy lasted all of a few months. After a weekend group trip to Amish country, Pennsylvania, it became apparent that, besides Jesus and pulsating hormones, we had nothing in common. I moved on.

For three years, the boys-verging-on-men in our youth group tried to convince me to "g" with one of them. Their flirtatious interactions with me would go nowhere because, whilst I liked the flirting, I did not want more from them. The most dismal of these attempted setups came from two elder brothers (Trevor and Curtis). Each were older than me and tried to set me up with their younger brothers (Peter and Randolph),[36] also a little older than me. Trevor was already occupied with another girl in the group and sought a match for his brother, Peter. This was not because their younger sibling developed genuine romantic affection for me, but because I was an unattached, reasonably attractive option in their proximity with built-in parental approval. Once again, I felt that the goal of these man-boys had nothing to do with who I was. At my emotional low, which corresponded with my most medically obese, I tried to convince myself that I should accept Peter's interest in me. I felt secure that being with him would not go down an unwanted sexual road. He was nearly twice my size. Though I have repeatedly found myself attracted to tall, thick, imposing men, Peter rung none of my bells. But I tried anyway, for a time, because I thought, as a girl, is this not what I am supposed to do? Cultivate a relationship with a Christian man who would one day marry me? Well-raised by Christian Jamaican parents to be chivalrous and kind, Peter was a perfectly fine boy. But I did not want him. With great effort, I pretended that I did. Well, I pretended to welcome his attention, never enthusiastically returning it, but careful not to rebuff it. The same was true for the other younger sibling, Randolph. This one went a little further because I allowed him to visit me in India for part of the holiday I took at the end of my three-month-long semester abroad program in Culture and Development. He was looking for adventure outside the United States and wanted to tag along for my plans. This was after his pursuit of me had somewhat cooled, having never matriculated to a relationship. I was twenty by that point, still grappling with allowing the needs and desires of men who wanted me to shape my response to them. I frequently went against my instinct to say "no", too haunted by childhood experiences of being perceived as selfish and mean to use "no" as a complete sentence. If I could not confidently explain my "no" back then, I chose excuses instead. Anticipating Randolph's impending visit to India, I made sure we would not be traveling alone. I had two other friends I met on the program join us—one woman and one man.

Today, both sets of brothers are married to Christian women with whom they have multiple children. I am happy that these men realized the life they wanted, or at least the one their faith requires of them. While I once thought being married to a man and having children was the inevitable outcome of being born female, that same thought seems foreign and limiting to me now. I would not change the tumultuous years of second-guessing my sexuality; the years I wrestled with allowing myself to yield to an internal guidance and curiosity rather than the hetero-patriarchal programming I had absorbed for so long. I would not change my life for the one I thought I would get, the one I was supposed to want.

The first time I recognized myself as being sexually attracted to someone, it was to the Black American man who would later become my ill-fated fiancé, Brian.[37] Brian's sonorous baritone resonated in every part of my body. He was also the first man (the only man) with whom I have ever been in love. Well-liked by guys and girls, Brian and I first met when he was eighteen and I was fifteen. I had a physical reaction to him almost instantly. He was kind to me, and we flirted, but as an overweight teenager, I never deluded myself that he would actually want me. He was charming with many girls who openly lusted after him. Though our romance would not start until I graduated college and moved back to DC, the wild cacophony of inescapable sensations when I was in his presence taught me what it felt like to desire someone—physically, intellectually, emotionally. His height, his build, his face, his voice were inseparable from his humor, intelligence, and sensitivity. Not only did I love to look at him, I loved being in conversation with him. Finally! What I saw on TV happening between two people was not just a trope I longed to be real. I felt its power without letting it overpower me. For me, Brian became the bar for how it should feel to want someone. To crave both their intellectual presence and their body. To think about them at night when you sinned, alone, underneath your sheets. Brian gave that to me, and I will forever remember him fondly for being who he was, and still is, and for helping translate reel to real.

7
The road to Queerville

When I graduated from Vassar College in May 2001, nothing significant happened a few months later, say in the month of September. Nothing that altered the world or led to the longest war in history. Nope. Just a perfectly ho hum autumn.

After my summer internship ended, it was not hard to find a full-time job, having graduated with an anthropology degree (with honors!). When I finally did get a job I liked, it was an economically insecure one with zero benefits. Two years later, I was still precariously employed and living in the family home. I imagined more for myself. Like so many college graduates in their twenties who lack direction, I decided that graduate school was the answer (or delay tactic) I needed. But the only thing I cared about at the time was cultural anthropology, and specifically Indian cultures. What I would do with a master's degree in Languages and Cultures of Asia, I did not know. I had not thought strategically about a five- or ten-year career plan, nor had I considered the job market limitations for a Black woman with such a master's degree. I was still plucky and independent, full of can-do and a delusional dose of "it will all work itself out".

University of Pennsylvania had been my first choice, but it was the University of Wisconsin-Madison that gave me a very rare master's program fellowship. And one that came with health and dental insurance! I could not pass that up. I had never had dental insurance. Ever. My family used Medicaid and the system of clinics for low-income people. By the time this dental insurance came along, my mouth was absent two molars which had been removed due to cavity rot. In 2003, when I started the program, I gleefully went to a dentist who gave me an industrial clean right after he told me I would need not one, two, three, but eight fillings! I would have to make two appointments to have four done each session. My time in Madison started with periodontal intervention and ended with mental health intervention.

I am grateful for the tuition-supported counseling services at both Vassar College and University of Wisconsin-Madison. Therapy was not something looked upon fondly, or well-understood in my own family, nor the Black Washington, DC area in which I grew up. On television, it seemed synonymous with white, upper-middle-class people; part of an over-thirty survival pack. Because I was surrounded by middle- and upper-class expectations at Vassar, I received encouragement to go to therapy when I was unable to contend with grief and depression my sophomore year.[38] I found it tremendously helpful, and still carry with me some of the revelations I unearthed there. Younger members of Generation X and millennials have pushed the mental health conversation out into the public sphere, beyond the comedic jokes about being neurotic and having a "shrink" that were pervasive in '80s and '90s media. One didn't have to be neurotic or in crisis to benefit from therapy. Today, it is much more commonplace to speak openly about mental health struggles than it was when I was younger.

By my final semester at UW-Madison, I was facing a slew of health problems, including adult onset of several new allergies. Even after blood tests, my doctor was having trouble pinpointing the cause of some of what ailed me. As one suggested change, he urged me to try stop taking birth control pills. The high hormone dosage of the prescription from my previous gynecologist made Doctor Turnbull uncomfortable. I was apprehensive. Given my fear of pregnancy, I had been religiously diligent about popping these pills. But, since I was spending several sexless months at a time away from my fiancée, that fear was nullified. The lack of artificial hormones helped lower my blood pressure, and … plot twist … boost my libido. When I began experiencing a raging sexual appetite for multiple men who were not my fiancé (who was back in DC),[39] I felt as if I were spinning out of control. So much was changing for me at that time, with life transitions I knew I would soon have to confront. The discipline I applied to completing my thesis was the only thing holding me together and keeping me on a timely track to graduation. I turned, once again, to counselling to help me unpack these intense emotions. At twenty-five, I felt like a teenage boy, ready to jerk off at the slightest suggestion of attraction. This seemingly indiscriminate lust was racially diverse in its targets, but always male. The gleaming white teeth of a sexy smile, muscular thighs, or wicked wit could easily tickle my loins at the time, triggering distracting daydreams and nighttime spasms. I had a hell of a fantasy life. None of this was cause for therapy. What worried me was the intense longing I directed at a classmate who, like myself, had a fiancée back at home.

Chris and I flirted all the time but I did not dare act on what I classed as good fun. However, inappropriate thoughts of him did lead me up many a mountain peak. On a night out with a bunch of grad students to celebrate the end of our program, Chris and I danced. Caught up in the energy of his closeness, I blurted out, in his ear, that I had a crush on him and wanted to have sex with him. He rejected me gently, reminding me how much he loved his fiancée. I was glad he was the adult because I was completely being led by my clitoris. Or so I thought. That incident with Chris led me to ponder what was wrong with me. Not the fantasies or randiness, but the fact that I propositioned Chris. That was reckless—the irresponsible cousin of intrepid, an adjective I did not associate with myself. Who is this girl? Was I prepared to reap the consequences of betraying the trust of my fiancé? I needed to get to the bottom of that compulsion. It took several weekly therapy sessions before I had a breakthrough. In a session just a week before graduation, I realized that my lust for Chris was not the problem, my relationship with Brian was. The long periods I endured without sex was the least of my relationship problems. I was not emotionally fulfilled and wanted I more; a more I feared I would never get with Brian. My reluctance to set a wedding date and complete disinterest in planning the event (despite books on the topic that Brian bought for me) were all indications that I did not want to be married. Not to Brian.

Within ten days of graduating with my master's degree and moving back to DC, I formally broke up with Brian. I don't recommend breaking up with someone in a public place (like a restaurant) unless the threat of violence from the person is very real. That was not a fear I had, and the logistics of the breakup were not well considered. It was just my luck that the Jasper's in which I had scheduled our break-up dinner was the same one in which Brian's younger sister was celebrating a promotion with her colleagues, mere feet from our table. I also forgot that I was the one to drive us there, so awkward is a cosmic understatement to describe the drive home. But the liberation I felt after dropping off Brian at his place was unparalleled. I felt higher than when my degree was conferred upon me; even more assured of my decision than when I had declined the PhD fellowship to the University of Chicago's Anthropology department two months before. I felt in charge of my life, in charge of my body. The summer of 2005 truly felt like every possibility awaited me.

Birthday dildo

Summer is my favorite season, partly because my birthday is in July. The sun's rays rejuvenate my soul, making me adventurous and frivolous. Upon turning twenty-six, I was newly single and I realize it had been five years since that was the case. I needed to get back in touch with myself and all the ways I had changed. The sexual charge I experienced from my hormonal reset (bye birth control pills!) lingered. To this, I did not object. The percolating desire had not changed, but my privacy had, now that I was confined to a single room in my grandmother's house. Though I lived alone in Madison, I was so broke that I never thought to purchase a sex toy—not online or in-store. I visited adult video stores on the outskirts of the city to rent or purchase XXX-rated DVDs a number of times, but never looked at the sex toys. When grandmother placed a $100 bill in my palm (her birthday gift to me), I used it to change that narrative.

Sex and the City, one of the most popular and provocative television shows of the late 1990s and early 2000s, brought "The Rabbit", a dildo with vibrating ears, out from its shameful pornographic shadows of the adult film industry and into mainstream conversations about the female orgasm. Featured on the show in one episode, and tried by all four characters, it was the prim and proper Charlotte who became "addicted" to the multiple orgasms that little rabbit-eared toy wrung from her. Whilst I was no stranger to self-induced orgasms, I wanted what Charlotte was having. I wanted to know what could possibly be so good as to compel me to ditch an evening out with my friends in favor of what that toy could offer (as Charlotte famously did). I knew exactly where to go to find that toy: *the* gayborhood of Washington, DC, Dupont Circle. Having spent many nights hanging with friends in that stylish and trendy part of DC, I passed the *Pleasure Chest*, an adult store, on many occasions but was too self-conscious to go inside. Being newly single had me feeling a little spicy. I marched in that store and bought myself a medium-quality "Rabbit" toy. It would be the first of many.

Looking back, purchasing the toy marked a significant moment in the development of my sexuality and sexual identity. Taking my pleasure in my own hands, so to speak, made me feel sexually secure. It was a major step for me as a Black woman in casting off shame. I had never discussed sex toys with any of my friends (Black or otherwise), and if they discussed it among themselves, they never told me. Had I not been bold enough to buy that toy,

I do not think I would have allowed myself to eventually marry a woman whom I would meet online months later.

The L Word made me queer ... maybe

The early spring night of 2005 that I happened upon a marathon of season two of Showtime's sapphic soap, *The L Word*, would change my life in ways I could not have anticipated. Ways that would lead me to sell my home and leave my beloved Washington, DC and a new job (that I loved!) at the Smithsonian to move to the mid-west equivalent of England. By the time I was back in DC, my affinity for *The L Word* (*TLW*) had turned into full fandom obsession. I hung out in online fan forums, consumed fan fiction, and occasionally contributed theories and scene analysis about the show. But, mostly, I lurked in the shadows. The *TLW* fan forum on Media Boulevard became ground zero for a major upheaval in my life. It was not fan chatter or the machinations of lesbian sex that became my most potent takeaway from the series; it was how it broadened my perspective on love and the fluidity of sexual identity.

I was a virgin when I entered Vassar, but by the time I left I had been kissed by a girl (without my consent, but with my enjoyment), had crushes on several others, and had entered into my first full sexual and romantic relationship with a man. But my sexual journey is not inseparable from my spiritual journey. Without the significant acceleration there, the sexual flame inside me could have no oxygen. Besides being one of the few white institutions in which I felt comfortably Black and nerdy, my time at Vassar was also the period during which I first questioned my heterosexual identity; not in a "gay until graduation" way (though there were plenty of sexual tourists and situational queers on campus). My queerness was both provoked and shuttered. The experiences I had during university would eventually lead me to understand that sexuality is not the rigid binary system I had been taught to uphold in the church. Sexuality can be fluid like a river, leading you through different landscapes if you choose to follow its flow.

It did not register, at the time, how many lesbians and queer people of color I surrounded myself with whilst at Vassar. One of them even married (and divorced) the girl in high school who had a crush on me! Others had sapphic relationships and later married men. Those women weren't necessarily exploiting gay women twenty years ago but, instead, trying to navigate their own tumultuous impulses. Of course, scientifically we know several things: (1) bisexuality is its own spectrum; (2) the porousness of female sexuality is far more acceptable and encouraged in society colored by patriarchy; (3) situational sexuality does exist, hence heterosexually inclined (or performing) men (and women) being capable of same-gender sexual relationships in restrictive or clandestine circumstances, such as prison or military organizations. Desires, be they food or sex, are not entirely naturalized, but are shaped by environment, availability, and socio-political mores.

I am not a lesbian, and neither is my wife

When I tell people that my wife and I met in an online forum for fans of *The L Word*, their assumptions run roughshod over the nerdy truth and unlikely reality behind our first acquaintance in late 2005. Neither of us were lesbians, nor had I ever had a sexual relationship with a woman. It would be almost two years before either of us could acknowledge and act on the queer feelings we developed for each other.

I have mild problem with numbers, a form of dyslexia where I confuse numbers (and, it turns out, acronyms). This condition led to Gillian and my first encounter. Before there were social media sites, like Tumblr, on which to blast our every feeling about TV, there were fan fora. These were early versions of what Reddit is today. *The L Word* forum on *Media Boulevard* is where Gillian and I unintentionally crossed paths at the end of 2005. Excited for *TLW*'s impending third season, I copied and pasted an expressive missive across several discussion topics on the forum. All of them contained the same jumbling of season three premiere date and acronym for the show (I had written "TWL"). Gillian piped up with a cryptic correction in one forum, which I defensively chose to interpret as snark. The attempted correction went over my head, and I returned a snappy public comeback. Twenty-four years my senior, she took a more mature approach and sent me a private message gently and clearly pointing to my mistakes. I took the correction in stride, making a joke of my mea culpa. From there a friendship was born.

Within months, our friendship grew beyond discussing the Showtime drama via PMs in the forum, and we graduated to email discussion. Eventually, we were comfortable enough to Skype with each other, and then to exchange phone numbers. The internet is a wild place full of dangerous people eager to exploit the young, who in turn are just searching for authentic human connection as they navigate the tumultuousness of adolescence. But I was an adult. I was honest with myself about my loneliness, something that had been brewing even during my engagement to Brian. To protect ourselves, we often build walls made of corrosive irony, biting humor, and cynicism, deploying these little arrows all over social media sites. Their pointy tips graze many who, already armored, are poised to forget about the attempted hit quickly. Rarely do any of those arrows make an impression, an indentation in the soft place on a person. Over the course of a year, I had removed my armor and Gillian burrowed into a soft place in me at a time when I was seeking to be seen, to be known.

Ours is a union that allows me to be myself. I don't feel like I have to perform anything for her—not my blackness, my femininity, nor my sexuality. Exclusively heterosexual until she met me, Gillian often likes to say she is Kadian-sexual. She is not attracted to women writ large, but I am not narcissistic enough to think she could never find another woman (or man) to make her happy. One of the smartest things I have ever done is to follow my instinct to love and to be loved by her, despite the chaos it would invite into my life.

There is a touch of naiveté about me that I have allowed to remain because it reminds me that I am human, fallible, with a streak of curiosity I may never let go of. It is that part of me that allowed myself to be open to a friendship with a white, English woman who was older than my mother. Gillian was the first friend I made on the internet, but not the last. I even made another friend from that same *TLW* forum who is still a card-carrying lesbian, one who lived ten miles from me and worked for USHMM at the time. What a small world.

Queer versus lesbian versus bisexual

In 2022, I watched a Channel 4 documentary entitled *Where Have All the Lesbians Gone?*[40] Focused on women-identified persons, the documentary asks what it means to be a lesbian in 2022, and why it is that young women who are sexually attracted to other women are choosing to identify as "queer" rather than "lesbian".[41] This was a matter of generational divide, with younger generations being more comfortable with "queer" than with "lesbian". Baby Boomers and most members of Generation X have grown up with "queer" as a derogatory, scarlet letter term, the only intent of which is to deride. For Millennials and Generation Z, "queer" is not an ugly term; it is a malleable one. Generational categories are arbitrarily constructed, but they are relevant in terms of the social, economic, and political climates that shape the outcomes of our lives. As a young member of Generation X (1979), I have a lot of things in common with Millennials, including my embrace of "queer" as an identity that fits much better than "lesbian".

After more than a decade, I had to distinguish for my heterosexual best friend, Alysia, the difference between identifying as a lesbian and identifying as queer—as I see it. She had been under the misapprehension for more than a decade that once things between Gillian and I had turned romantic, it meant I had become a lesbian. I am not now, nor have I ever been, a lesbian. Lesbians are women-identified people who desire and participate—almost exclusively—in romantic relationships with other women. Gillian is not the first woman to whom I've been attracted, but she is the first with whom I have desired to pursue a romantic relationship. My sexual attraction to those who are not women endures. Penises still excite me, but my titillation isn't dependent on their presence. Were Gillian and I ever to part ways, I would consider another same gender relationship, but I would be open to other types, too—whatever their gender or sexual orientation. This lack of fixity is what I enjoy about being queer. I am not interested in narrowing that further in order to fit into a neat box.

Some may question the difference between bisexuality and queerness. Bisexuality, despite appearing flexible, has a binary problem. Sexuality and gender identity are two distinct spectrums that sometimes intersect, but they are not one and the same. "Bi", meaning sexuality oriented to two genders, does not fit with the understanding of gender being a spectrum. It is an outdated term tied to gender binaries. I don't begrudge those who hold onto that identity, especially if their ideas about men and women are fixed. Mine no longer are, and so "bisexual" is not a term that fits my identity. The freedom that "queer" enables me to express in gender and sexuality is more my cup of tea. But, you know, enjoy whatever kind of tea makes your pot boil.

Queer as a ... choice

Sociologists, psychologists, journalists, and others have spent the last few decades advancing the scientific legitimacy of homosexuality, not just among humans, but as an orientation evidenced throughout the animal kingdom. Debates over sexuality in the scientific community now lean toward there being genetic coding responsible for homosexual inclinations, but this was not always the case. Sexual proclivity is a spectrum full of complex facets. There was a time in the not-too-distant past when homosexuality was regarded as a genetically programmed inevitability or predilection, one that man-made interventions could not completely undo. This interpretation blew up religious and moral condemnations of gayness as a sinful choice or unfortunate disease. But codifying homosexuality as genetic also diminishes some of the sociological complexity between the hetero- and homo-polarities of sexuality. It is possible to have an active choice in our sexuality. We can be overwhelmingly oriented in one sexual direction and dabble in others. A gay man kissing or having sex with a woman does not make him a heterosexual. Neither do two men kissing necessarily *make* them gay. In his essay "Queer is a Verb", sexual educator Charlie Glickman (2012), notes that of the many things queer can mean, it is also a verb that allows us to push at boundaries, question assumptions, and examine biases. To be queer is more than mathematical arrangements of genitalia and gender; it is also a mindset and approach to living life in less restrictive ways.[42]

When it comes to categorizing its language, sexuality, like gender, is not fixed. Consider how Black Americans have reappropriated the racist term "n*gger", transforming it into "n*gga", which can be adapted as a gender-inclusive noun, adverb, verb, or adjective. When used *intra*-racially among Black people, it can express camaraderie and inclusivity, or be used to insult and alienate, depending on context, tone, and other factors. "N*gga" is one the most fluid and descriptive terms in AAVE. The term "queer" has been developing along similar lines over the last twenty years in terms of malleability. Queer is a way of expressing one's dis-identification with heterosexuality without committing to an equally confining new identity. Queer is its own spectrum.

Where the boundaries of heterosexuality are stiff and rigid, queer's boundaries are elastic, enabling you to push against them and find a place for yourself. In our over-saturated social media environment, there is a trend toward hyper-identification and micro-categorization. This is a move toward labelling everything one is, does, or enjoys. Cynically, this micro-labelling serves hashtag algorithms of media platforms looking to shovel more content and relevant ads at its customers just as much as it facilitates communication between people. These tags help us to better externally categorize who we are for the sake of other people's consumption of us (we're more searchable), but such labels don't necessarily help us *be* who we are. They help us perform the identities we ascribe to the aestheticization of identity.

As an anthropologist-cum-sociologist, I know that definitions are important, especially when it comes to forming communities and providing resources for the cohesion of said communities. We live in an age of extreme individualization that is worrisomely being combined with branding practices that are turning individuals into human corporate entities; ones who are driven in this direction because extreme wealth inequality has left them with fewer options for creating financial security. Living in this era of economic precarity that is tied to marketing on media platforms owned by a handful of companies makes it harder to distinguish between authenticity and that which is simply marketable performance. In other words, I am growing cynical. When I am watching a TikTok video, it is hard to know if I am watching a person being their authentic self or if they are playing to what is algorithmically more likely to get consumed (views, likes, clicks). I know the truth is unsettlingly somewhere in between. It is impossible to precisely quantify the degree to which we are shaping technology with our experience and how much it is shaping us as it learns our patterns of behavior and spits them back out at us in marketable ways.

Fleeing the "free-est" country in the world

I often get asked by British people what made me want to move to the UK from a country like the United States. What on earth would possess me to move from such a land of plenty, of innovation and consumer options? These people are often white, but not exclusively. Often heterosexual. Often lacking the connection between the American political polarization they watch via the news and Twitter timelines and the real people those politics affect. Many people did not realize that before 2015, the United States did not have federal marriage equality. They did not know that the Defense of Marriage Act (DoMA) had existed since 1996, limiting marriage to opposite gender couples. Part of this lack of understanding comes from conflating liberal American TV shows with the political reality under which its citizens live. Moreover, many outside the United States do not fully understand how the country's federalism (individual state-based authority) functions; that marriage could be defined state by state, but also upheld under national laws. Long before the Supreme Court ruled in *Obergefell v. Hodges* (2015) that same sex couples were guaranteed the fundamental right to marry, according to both the due process and equal protection clauses of the Constitution's fourteenth Amendment, Gillian and I were dubious anything would legally change for us whilst living in DC. We gave up hope seven years before the Supreme Court's ruling.

For almost two years, Gillian was a glorified visitor, going back and forth each month between the UK and Washington, DC, where we tried to make a life between plane rides. We made a great life for ourselves in a beautiful, modern two-bedroom condo in DC's Meridian Hill neighborhood. We joined a gay volunteering group (Burgundy Crescent), traveled, made friends, and hosted dinner parties. Our life was full in DC, and I loved it. The only thing missing was immigration stability for Gillian. One of the things denied to me as a United States citizen under marriage inequality was the right to obtain a fiancée visa for Gillian, which would then allow us to marry. Immigration was processed at the federal level, despite a smattering of United States states (including our non-state of Washington DC) legalizing gender-inclusive marriage. The federal government did not recognize our relationship as legitimate. If we were wealthy and had a spare $500,000 at the time to invest in the United States economy, we could have sought a resident visa for Gillian. Alternatively, she could have founded a church as another pathway to a visa. I wish I were joking (see Chapter 6).

When Barack Obama ran for president in 2008, we grew hopeful that maybe the tide was turning. On a glorious, unseasonably warm November night we literally danced our way up U Street as we walked home from our neighborhood gay bar, *Nelly's*, celebrating Barack Obama's win as the country's 44th president and 1st Black president. We hugged each other and random people on the street who reached out to express their joy. What a time! It was a night you had to have lived through to understand.

We were … hopeful. Obama's win seemed like a silver lining in a dark sky. That is, until the next morning, when we woke up and learned that Proposition 8 had passed in California. Before it was ruled unconstitutional in federal court in 2010, Proposition 8 was a ballot initiative in California which attempted to amend the state's constitution to ban same sex marriage. Though we lived in Washington, DC, California often set the progressive agenda for the rest of the United States. The cold, stark reality of Proposition 8's passage hit us that next morning, making it dubious we would ever be able to settle in the United States as a couple.

We were already married when Barack Obama was elected. Well, we had a civil partnership. With the exception of Northern Ireland, the United Kingdom began allowing same sex unions in December 2005. As a compromise with the Church of England, civil unions afforded all the legal protections of marriage, but the term "civil union" was to be used to protect the "hetero-sanctity" of marriage whilst also granting secular legal protections afforded to married persons. Barf. Eye roll. We got "married"[43] in a little town in Scotland called Annan, in a register office, by a woman named Shirley. We picked Scotland for administrative convenience,[44] not because Gillian is half Scottish. The UK had a less rigid immigration system for its citizens who wished to be joined by their non-British partner. Once civil unions were approved for same gender couples only,[45] it meant that they could take advantage of immigration pathways for their partners. I applied for a marriage visa in early 2008; we were married by that June. The honeymoon was in Greece.

Our civil union meant nothing in the eyes of many legal entities in the United States, a thing we knew. But we protected our relationship in the British legal system in case things became untenable in the United States and we would have to move. I am writing in very unromantic terms about our marriage because the impetus behind it was not romantic at all, on the surface. Our bond was already solidified, and we could not imagine a life in which we were not together. It was not the relationship that we questioned, but its perceived lack of value under United States law. We mattered to each other, but we knew we did not matter to America. We had to protect ourselves by any means necessary.

The first ominous sign came one spring day in 2009 when Gillian arrived at Dulles airport after a routine trip back to the UK for work. She was told by an immigration officer that "The [90-day] visa waiver system is not meant for this kind of frequent traveling". After traveling between both countries every six to eight weeks for nearly two years, Gillian was told that she would have to apply for an official ten-year visa. She would have to go for the appointment at the United States Embassy in London. I drove Gillian to Dulles International Airport the night of our first wedding anniversary so that she could attend her visa appointment. She would never return to our DC home.

I will never forget how nonchalantly I answered the phone days later when her phone number popped up. I was in my shared office at the Smithsonian's National Museum of Natural History when Gillian's phone call changed the trajectory of my life. Of our lives. Gillian was inconsolable on the other line, which disoriented me. I had taken the outcome of her visa appointment to be a foregone conclusion. The interview would be a mere formality.

"They rejected me", she cried. And I didn't hear her at first. I could not absorb the unexpected outcome.

"What?!"

"I said they rejected me. There was no interview. They said I didn't have strong enough ties to Britain".

Her job was there. Her family was there. Her sons. Her accounts. So much of her life. Of everything, I was her only tie to the United States. What great irony that they saw me as her most significant tie to the United States and therefore used it as a reason to separate her from me. I was too shocked by this news to cry or even be angry. The panic was rising inside me, but I did not let it out. I am not getting divorced, I thought. Having been a veteran of navigating our relationship on the back end of a five-hour time difference, there was no way I was going to have a long-distance marriage. My new job, my family, our condo—all if it flashed before me.

"Well, that means I'll have to move there".

I said it without significant deliberation. It seemed the most logical thing, given the circumstances. The practical and emotional weight of the decision was a matter that only time and experience would later reveal to me. But in that basement office on that June day, I was going to do whatever I needed to live with Gillian. I was not going to give up that kind of love for the United States, who never loved me back. My family would have to understand. My job (one I adored and was excellent at) ... I would figure that out. And I did. The Smithsonian has been very good to me. Ten months later, Gillian and I were reunited permanently in England. And though queer relationships now enjoy legal standing in the United States, I have no plans to resettle there. Gillian and I bought a home, adopted two dogs, and created a full life for ourselves in the UK. Besides, I have reinvented myself as a university lecturer and entrepreneur.[46] Twenty years ago, I had not pictured either career. Living abroad, being married to a woman, none of that was on my Bingo card. Twenty years ago, I was still afraid of dogs, and now I am obsessively dedicated to my two furry darlings, Bobigny (Parisian arrondissement) and Livvie (a diminutive for Olivia (Pope)). My life is nothing like I could have imagined as a teenage girl. I am so fortunate.

8
Love as a mission

"Love's Lover"

"Love's Lover" is proudly displayed in my Twitter profile. Sitting alongside a host of other identifiers (jobs I hold, political stances), "love's lover" is, arguably, the least tangible one listed. It is, however, the identifier I hold most dear because it is my guiding light through every storm; a navigational tool for my ever-evolving self. I love being a woman who is Black. However, female and Black were assigned to me.[47] Lovingly embraced to be sure, both those identities were ones whose permutations I learned to understand. Love, too, is like this. We tend to naturalize or treat love as a passive phenomenon to which we "fall" prey. No. It is very active. It is something we learn, cultivate, give, and live. Love is a verb. I cannot recall a time without love. I grew up in a family where, though there were deficiencies, love was instinctive, an axiomatic driver providing safety, affection, and protective guardrails. Love was told and shown. This does not mean I was without trauma or misfortune no child should have to face.

Once she reached America, mother, whose adolescence was placed on pause, indulged in every tempting opportunity that eluded her as a young mother of two in Jamaica. My younger brother remained with his father in Jamaica, and I was safely ensconced with my grandparents. I was abandoned by my mother, first as a child while she cavorted with drug dealers in the late 1980s, and then later by her imprisonment throughout most of the 1990s. It has taken a lot of work as an adult to form an identity and sense of self that is more than a collection of traumas. I am more than the things that have happened *to* me.

My grandparents were mostly ships in the night, but not until I was in high school. In my primary school years, the adults in my family worked day shifts. My grandfather's mother and older sister lived across the street from my elementary school. My great grandmother looked after several children in the basement until my grandparents or my aunt Arlene came home between five and six o'clock to pick us up from my great aunt's house. The great aunt who owned this house was the same one with whom my grandparents lived when they first arrived in America. Aunt Meeks, as we called her, had a husband, Uncle Cover, who was frequently stumbling around in a stench-cloud of stale alcohol. I cannot remember if he worked at all, or if that was left solely to his wife. Maybe he was retired by then. I do remember that on at least two occasions, he managed to sequester me, while my great grandmother was upstairs, long enough to molest me. I know that I was not the only child he violated. I said nothing for a very long time. By the time I was about ten years old, and a much older cousin confronted the family about our great uncle's assault against her, I made up my mind never to tell any of my family. They did not believe Cousin Camille. Many of the extended family performed mental gymnastics so that they could defend her molester. Camille was ostracized from the family after that because seeing her reminded them of what their husband, father, brother-in-law, uncle was: a pedophile. Camille was living evidence of his crime. Without her around, they could easily forget who and what Uncle Cover was: a pedophile. I knew I did not want to experience what Camille endured, especially being ten years her junior.

My uncle, Michael, who arrived from Jamaica about a year after my mom and I did, was the only person to approach me after Camille's revelation to the family. He sat me down and talked to me about which kinds of touches were OK and the ones that were not. He told me that if I had been or ever should be touched inappropriately, I should go to him so that he could protect me. Even with this promise from him, I did not possess the courage to tell him he was too late. It already happened. Camille was an adult when she told the family; I was a child who still had to be around the very same people who denied her reality. What if I had told my uncle and everyone else denied what happened to me? I would not take the risk of being betrayed. My little heart could not handle the potential disappointment of being disbelieved by the immediate family members I loved. Even with my uncle's promise, what if he, too, became influenced by the inevitable criticism from our extended family? In Uncle Cover's abuse, I knew I was not special, and I did not conceive that my confession would absolve anything; not after what I witnessed happen with Camille. But I promised my uncle I would tell him if I faced any future transgressions. Promises are more easily spoken than kept.

I was in my early twenties before I would confess to my mother what Uncle Cover did to me. She was living in Croydon then as an undocumented immigrant. She wept into her bath water. So long was her wailing, her bath grew cold. She attempted to take responsibility, noting that had she not been "ripping and running" the streets with drug dealers at that time, perhaps she could have been the one caring for me and her youngest sister after school. Perhaps. Perhaps. Perhaps. I did not blame her, however, nor anyone else in my family except for the one who committed the crime. I was fortunate to have two years of counselling covered by my tuition scholarship at Vassar, which helped me unpack my great-uncle trauma. Internally, I had grieved and processed what happened to me during those years. I was fortunate to move on. No man would destroy me. To this day I have not told my grandmother, and unless she reads this, I am not going to. It is not because I am hiding from it but because it doesn't matter to me anymore. I no longer hold it close.

I know that had the adults in my life been able to collect me from school, or at least be at home when I was a child, the molestation would not have happened. But, realistically, they had to work, and my great grandmother's childcare services cost a pittance in comparison to professional services. Defining love—its manifestation and receptions—is rarely a pure thing, not in a society heavily shaped by experiences with gender, race, class, sexuality, among other factors. Our parental figures were not only contending with their personal demons or inadequacies, but also ones forced upon them. These are some of the ways in which I would come to understand these complexities as an adult looking at life in the rear-view mirror. It took a lot of therapy and growing up before I could find grace for my mother's choices separately from how they affected my adolescence. "Mother" was not her only identity. She is a whole person independent of me or my brother. Even with the gaping mother wound, sporadically engaged father, and experience of sexual abuse, I never felt completely abandoned or unloved. There was always someone left to care for me. Confronting and processing deficits of the past have helped shaped my outlook on loving—not as a something pristine and tidy, but something honest. Love is something I want to live and give in ways that are authentic to who I am. That person is partly shaped by the things I have experienced, the ways I have seen love function (and dysfunction). But I am still a person in the making, and so is my love.

Taking love seriously

I was exposed to pornography (see Chapter 5) years before consuming a regular diet of Hollywood's romantic tropes. Watching soap operas such as *All My Children* and *General Hospital*, tucked into my grandmother's side, provided me with a Hollywood introduction to romantic love stories (and white treachery, my favorite genre). The stories of romance resonated with me, even though, as a child, I did not completely understand them, nor the ways in which their tropes were subconsciously shaping what I imagined to be the trajectory of a woman's life. Until my mid-twenties, I imagined romantic love could only go one way for me—a husband and children. I thought Brian was going to be the man helping realize this romantic fantasy. I ignored his tendencies to shrug off basic adult responsibilities, and how he cut off communication with me when he experienced bouts of both sadness and what I suspect was depression. I had been contending with anxiety and depression since I was a teenager, and Brian would be there for me during my low times if I reached out to him. But he disallowed this reciprocity for himself. This was a manifestation of his male ego and the ways he had been taught to cope with vulnerability. He did not want me to see him in that way.

We all have blind spots that cause us to be truculent or insensitive. Those things shape our communication skills. When Brian experienced emotional unease, he shuttered himself away. As an adult, one's mental health is still one's responsibility. Even when we are in pain or enduring chemical imbalance, we remain accountable for our actions and attitudes towards others. The actions we take belong to *us* and it is our duty to ourselves to seek help when we need it.[48] That is a tough pill to swallow for me, too. The final straw with Brian was when he did not show up for my graduation from UW-Madison. His plane ticket had already been booked but he did not board the plane. The day before he was to fly to Madison, he called me. A lost wallet in a CVS. No cash on hand. He did not think he could make it. To me this was a minor inconvenience and not the barrier Brian made it out to be.

"But you have your passport, which is all you need to get on the plane. Metro to Reagan Airport, and I've got you once you're here. You'll be with me. There's food here, and I've already booked dinner for after the ceremony. There's nothing you need money for during your trip. You'll have your bank card back by the time you get home". I tried to be reasonable but was incredulous that he was seriously considering not coming to my graduation.

"This is a big weekend for you. I don't want to meet your father looking like a bum. I can't pay for nothing. How's that going to look?" Brian defended.

I was thinking logically. He was thinking symbolically, specifically of how his cash-lessness, as a man, would be interpreted as an inability to be a provider as my future husband. I have a family full of women, but the only member Brian mentioned was my father, whom he had not met before. The great irony in all of this was that I grew up with both grandparents working and agreeing that my grandmother would be the financial head of the household. My father had a long history of sometimes needing to lean financially on women. He was not prideful about this. So, when I told him he would not be meeting my fiancé this time, as he had expected, I did not make up an excuse for Brian. I was honest, and told him that Brian lost his wallet and, as a result, did not feel comfortable joining us. My father expressed a disappointment in Brian's choice that made clear for me the reoccurring battle I would have with him should our marriage proceed. The revelation was that Brian's pride would always come before my emotional needs. The thought of future battles with him about the same thing exhausted me whilst I watched my family eat and laugh during the post-ceremony dinner.

I felt a peace wash over me that weekend as I became certain I would end my relationship with Brian, not just the engagement. The love my family and friends surrounded me with that weekend made me realize I should not accept anything less from a man, especially from one who claimed to want to make a lifelong commitment to me. That's hustling backwards. Love is the commitment, not the marriage contract. One of my favorite flawed heroines, Bette Porter, from The L Word (2005), in an episode that aired a few months before my graduation, gave a toast to two engaged women. Her powerful words were still lodged in my brain, in my heart:

> [To] caring, kindness and trust, longevity and respect.
> To all the things that you'll need to keep your love alive.
> I wish you happiness. And I hope that you forever spare each other pain.

Having now been married for fourteen years, I know that sparing each other pain is impossible, but loving someone means trying your best to avoid that pain and taking responsibility for when you are the cause of their pain. There is much I could write about the ways in which Brian's decision is indicative of a sort of toxic masculinity that has reduced men's value to providing financial and physical security. When they fall short of that, they feel resentful and disconnected from their purpose, which then negatively impacts their ability to emotionally connect in relationships. This form of patriarchy is a serious barrier to taking love seriously, and it is one that men (and the women who have naturalized patriarchal expectations) must be vigilant about.

Love as a commitment

Romantic love is but one small aspect of loving, though it is the one with which our culture is most obsessed. I understand why. I, too, have consistently consumed romantic media of all sorts since childhood. But as a concept and reality, love is undervalued because of its perception as the purview of the feminine. Frivolous, soft, emotional, optional—all are terms we associate with "feminine". I once took a course at Vassar entitled "Love". It was cross-listed in the Religion and Philosophy departments.

The professor—a Native American man—covered the different concepts of love. I recall being shocked that such a class was offered. It was a sign to me that the topic was a legitimate field of study, one of both reason and emotion. Today, I teach a second-year undergraduate course entitled "Black Feminism(s)", and in it I make the topic of love and its connection to blackness and liberatory movements an explicit topic. It is my way of helping my young students to see love's seriousness, its expansiveness as something more than the basis for the manipulative reality dating shows saturating our media. In the lecture on love, I combine excerpts from bell hooks' (2012) *All About Love*[49] with contemporary lyrics from the Carters' (Beyoncé and Jay-Z) album, *Everything is Love*; specifically, the song "Black Effect" (The Carters, 2018). I use it to prompt a discussion about love of one's community as a key part of cultural authenticity. Without it, one's blackness is merely affect without true effect.

Loving blackness

Much of African-American culture has been created and endured because of an indomitable spirit that, despite every attempt at destruction or reduction, finds ways to keep creating art, innovating on the English language, and loving themselves and each other. One of the whackest things about white supremacy is how its parasitic nature, one in constant need of an oppressed other, has convinced some that gatekeeping Black culture is necessary, or even possible. I should say *attempt* to gatekeep Black culture because none of us individually own it, but it is ours to create, shape, disseminate, and pass on to future generations. Gates keep people out, but also in. This communal stake in culture is anathema to the principles of the white capitalist patriarchal supremacy, which sees value in something only once it can be manipulated for capital gain. As Black people we have grown up in a society infused with these values, and many of our educational institutions naturalize them.

We cannot draw boundaries around our art and culture in the ways we've attempted with race, gender, and sexuality (things that aren't binary anyway). Artistic expression of Black American culture—be it language, food, media, movement, and so on—deserve recognition and respect. In one of my favorite media review podcasts, *This Too Much* (Ikpi and Morrow, 2022), co-hosts Rod Morrow and writer Bassey Ikpi engage in thoughtful discussions about themes present in their favorite TV shows. In one about the TV show *Atlanta*, they discussed nuances of cultural appropriation and Black art that were largely absent from social media discourse on the topic. Bassey says that the nature of art is to be generative—it is supposed to give birth to more art. Rod says "cultural appropriation" is over diagnosed to the point it has lost meaning. Conversations about it have strayed far from its implications around power, theft, and co-option for financial gain. If legal claims could be exercised, do we not think that individual West and Central African tribes would have claim to this culture which has been influenced by them as the bedrock of all blackness? That Caribbean cultures, Jamaican DJs, do not have some claim to American hip-hop? Copyright, trademark, and intellectual property rights are legal markers to legitimize ownership and protect financial interest. They are, of course, useful to many people to protect property and financial interests. Black culture(s) cannot be owned because culture is a living, evolving thing, not a legal thing.

African-American culture is the greatest unacknowledged global export of the United States. Black diasporic interpolations of African cultures have been moving people, and influencing culture, art, music, and fashion around the globe for centuries and continues to do so. Where they used to be regional exchange, influences have morphed into something with global significance because of increased connectivity resulting from economic, social, and political globalization. In the digital age, influence moves even faster, spreads even wider. Yes, that leaves us open to greater cultural exploitation and appropriation when what we want to do is protect our creations, but to think that any one of us, or any designated group or organization, could somehow gatekeep Black cultural influence is not just a pipe dream; it more closely resembles coloniality than liberation.

One impetus behind wanting to erect protective boundaries around blackness is the fear of exposure. We fear that Black culture is made vulnerable when it is made too accessible to white people. The notion that "Representation Matters" is a double-edged sword because when we generate stories and art that reflect the authenticity of our Black lives, we are also exposing ourselves to everyone else for consumption. Clearly that is the nature of media, but my point here is that to depict Black life is also to expose it, and there are downsides to that. There is a mystique in imagining ourselves to be as opaque and unknowable as the color after which we call ourselves. It is partly for this reason that minority communities sometimes fervently reject representations of ourselves even when we are informed by creators who are part of our community, which is bound to happen because Black experiences are diverse. By cataloguing and preserving Black cultural experiences, we protect the recipes, if you will. Colonialism systematically codified the "supremacy" of whiteness through the vilification and denigration of Black people and our cultures, the distorted images of which were commodified and sold back to us. Black became everything synonymous with decline, insolence, and undesirability. As a result, many of us have internalized a level of shame around parts of Black cultures, which is not our fault. A systematic attempt to dislodge pride in ourselves will do that to a people.

But it *is* our responsibility to examine the prick of shame we feel when it rears its ugly head; our responsibility to interrogate that shame's productivity in our lives. Shame masquerades often as anger because the latter *feels* more powerful and righteous than the former, even when it's ultimately more destructive. Each year, during Black History Month, when a university cafeteria serves some food representative of and enjoyed by African-Americans—say watermelon salad[50]—it is not simply anger that people feel about being stereotyped, but also a deeply internalized, learned shame around a piece of fruit; a piece of fruit that, in the late 19th and early 20th centuries, were symbols of financial entrepreneurship in African-American communities. It is white supremacy which turned that symbol of pride and progress, the watermelon, into caricatured advertisements and a point of Black mockery. Reclaim the watermelon. It's delicious, especially alongside delicious fried chicken: a very satisfying, low-carb meal. Love and acknowledge where our culture comes from, or don't. Either way it is not going to force white people to see us any differently. They have never needed our permission to deny us love, even as they remain fascinated with the culture Black people create.

Love and capitalism: an experiment

Scholars I admire, like the late bell hooks, have written extensively on why capitalism is antithetical to something like love because the former is structured around domination and the latter is liberatory in its most authentic form. They don't mix. I agree with hooks, ostensibly. But I am experimenting with how successful I can be with love as a founding value of a capitalist pursuit. *How far in business can I get before, potentially, sacrificing that value for greater financial gain? If I move on a sign, will it be because of failure or clarity?* These are just some of the questions I consider as an ethical business owner.

What started as fun hobby intended to result in a useable solution for my dry, tangled coily hair in 2014 turned into a low stakes "side hustle" by 2017.[51] What eventually became Bourn Beautiful Naturals (now rebranded as BB Naturals (BBN)) today, a solutions-based brand catering to those with textured hair and sensitive skin, began as a psychological haven away from the taxing demands of my PhD. When I started the PhD program, I was working three jobs to fund it (before I earned a bursary to study). I was tired all the time and my research was muddled, intangible, and dispiriting. The creams I was creating in my garage had a more immediately satisfying outcome. I could see the fruits of my effort, assess where I went wrong, and adjust my formula or process to get a better result. When I began to get really good results and amass a host of solutions for my Black hair and sensitive skin needs, I gave away those potions to friends and family. I was surprised these creations turned out to be a hit, primitive as they seemed back then. The first person to see communal and financial value in them was my friend Nicole Andrews. She offered to pay me for several products, which she then distributed to her family and friends for feedback. She brought the consensus back to me, along with her own request for a hair solution for her children that she could not find on the market. Nicole was such a loving, beautiful person, generous in spirit, and smart as a whip. I was lucky to have her friendship and her confidence as a fellow PhD scholar at the time. I worked diligently to create something effective that Nicole also felt safe using on her children's hair. Wax and petroleum products were just two of the things she wanted excluded in a modern day "hair grease". The product I eventually created ("Hair Too Balm") was beloved by Nicole, her husband, and her children. She remained a customer until her untimely death in 2022, due to complications with secondary (brain) cancer, after surviving breast cancer. I tell that story because were it not for Nicole, I don't think I would have taken my hobby public. Nicole saw the potential, not in BB Naturals, but in me. I worked hard to see what she saw in me. It took a year of Leaning Back for me to see what she saw. The same love that I put into creating products for myself, for Nicole and other Black women, which now comprise the BB Naturals line, is something I am determined to keep at the foundation of my business. Because that love is what inspires my purpose.

Practically, what does it mean to have love as a guiding principle in business? It means centering Black people as my default customer, not an "other", in the language I use to describe my products and in the images used to represent those products. It means not marketing to Black women in a way that tries to convince them that their hair and their bodies are a problem that only my products solve. It means not using ingredients that will harm their hair or skin simply because those ingredients are affordable or frequently used in the beauty industry. It means not using colonial language like "frizzy", "tame", or "hard to manage" on haircare products. Because Black hair is not a problem that needs to be solved; the society which demands we subordinate ourselves to beauty standards created in opposition to our bodies is the problem. And it means that I don't lie to women by saying that a single product is going to grow their hair or solve hair loss when I know those issues are immunology related.

I could have a good teaching career, write books, and let that be that. I'm not in denial or deluded. Of course, I want this business endeavor to be successful enough to give me financial security. But that motivation cannot be the only driving factor for this pursuit. Without keeping my love alive for serving the needs of Black people of all genders, the pure pursuit of capitalism is fundamentally uninteresting to me. At some point, this conviction may be challenged when BB Naturals is exposed to a larger consumer base. I hope I have the courage to keep my values close to my vest, to be able to live with myself for the decisions I make, and to love myself through the challenges of maintaining my convictions.

Notes

Introduction

1. Katrinapavela.tumblr.com

1 Welcome to America

2. Kingston, the capital of Jamaica, was not a major tourist destination city, unlike Ocho Rios, Negril, Port Royal.

3. Jamaicans and other Caribbean islanders use the term "cool" when describing someone's skin tone as brown. That is, the person does not have "too much" or "too little" melanin. It can also refer secondarily to the clarity of the person's skin.

2 Learning to be Black and female in America

4. According to the strategic plan outlined in 2003. www.brooki ngs.edu/wp-content/uploads/2016/06/20030417_revitali zingdc_williams.pdf

5. The Chris Darden (Sterling K. Brown) character in *American Crime Story* (2016).

6. According to the US Department of Education, the "National Blue-Ribbon School award affirms the hard work of students, educators, families, and communities in creating safe and welcoming schools where students master challenging and engaging content. The National Blue-Ribbon School flag gracing an entry or flying overhead is a widely recognized symbol of exemplary teaching and learning". The program began giving awards in 1983.

7. I will never forget when, in 2017, a group of HBCU presidents visited Trump's Oval Office, in symbolic prostration, for federal funds to support their institutions. They were invited because Trump was to sign an executive order benefiting HBCUs. The White House Initiative on HBCUs was moved from its place in the Department of Education directly to the White House in order to give the program "more clout within the government" (Strauss and Mathews, 2017). The February 2017 executive order, signed by Donald Trump, did not, however, earmark any specific amount of funding for HBCUs. In the end, the 2017–2020 "Contributions Brief" notes that the Initiative was given an allocation budget of a mere $130,000 (Holifield, 2021).

8. Hillman University was the fictitious HBCU portrayed in the TV show, *A Different World*.

9. The Netflix documentary *High on the Hog* does an excellent job of detailing the culinary contributions of enslaved and free Black Americans, and the relationships between their diasporic cuisine and specific West African food traditions.

10. I interviewed Yvonne and several of her cohorts from Sarah Lawrence about their activism in the 1960s and 1970s. Some of their perspectives are featured in "Be Who You Are: Black Feminism in Volatile Realities", in *The Fire Now: Anti-racist Scholarship in Times of Racial Violence,* edited by Azeezat Johnson, Remi-Joseph Salisbury, and Beth Kamunge, 2018, University of Chicago Press/Zed Books.

11. Banneker required all students to accrue 300 supervised hours of volunteering to graduate high school. This was three times the amount required by most DC public schools.

3 Black liberation, who? Black liberation, what?

12. Hall's data draws on statistics from the United Kingdom, but his thesis is equally appliable to the United States as blackness functions as a synonym for criminal in both countries.

13. Meaning "peace on him" in Hebrew.

14. She eventually earned her Graduate Equivalent Diploma (GED) whilst in federal prison.

15. "It's Handled" (2013). *Scandal*. 3.01. ABC Network. 3 October.

16. An ethics-based training administered by the museum to local and national law enforcement, including FBI recruits and in-service officers. It aims to give law enforcement a perspective on their place in society and the consequences of their actions in upholding policies unjust to some communities.

4 White supremacy is whack

17. West, Crissle (2014). "Lemon Pepper Wings", *The Read*. Loud Speakers Network. 8 May 2014. Podcast.

18. The 13th Amendment in the United States Constitution outlaws slavery but allows incarcerated people to be subjected to involuntary labor.

19. Written by Jordan Temple, of Trinidadian heritage.

20. I interviewed African-American and Black British women who were politically active in the 1960s and 1970s, respectively.

21. According to CNN's 2016 exit polls https://edition.cnn.com/election/2020/exit-polls/president/national-results.   Other polls have indicated lower results (fifty-two to fifty-four percent), but still a plurality.

22. According to Jane Junn, Professor of Political Science at the University of Southern California, who wrote about white women's very long history of being in step with white patriarchy.   http://politicsofcolor.com/white-women-vote-republican/

23. According to a 2009 report by the Pew Research Center: www. pewresearch.org/hispanic/2009/04/30/dissecting-the-2008-electorate-most-diverse-in-us-history/

24. Of the racial ethnic groups, when examined across the male gender, those identifying as Black are the least likely to vote Republican, yet a worrying eighteen percent swung for Trump in 2016. Perhaps Tawny's husband was among them. If so, a pox on him, too.

25. Taken from Baldwin's infamous 1965 televised Cambridge debate with William F. Buckley Jr. https://www.youtube.com/watch?v=NUBh9GqFU3A

26. Freire, P. 1970. *Pedagogy of the Oppressed*. New York. Continuum Press.

5 Ex-church girl

27. Two decades later, she would get her GED in Alderson Prison.

28. Here, I am referring to the disrespect and discrimination shown to transgender men.

29. Thirty-year study of murder rates in Washington, DC. https://ocme.dc.gov/sites/default/files/dc/sites/ocme/publication/attachments/APPENDIX%20A%20-%2030%20year.pdf

30. This is invented and the real name repressed.

31. This name, too, is invented and the real memory repressed.

32. In 1990, Congress amended the Immigration and Nationality Act to add "religious worker" as an eligibility criterion to establish permanent residency in the USA. Note that the language is written in terms of Christianity, though not expressly stated. www.uscis.gov/green-card/green-card-elig ibility/green-card-for-a-religious-worker-minister-or-nonm inister

33. I know that those who do not identify as women can also become pregnant and are thus detrimentally affected by these theocratic laws. The intention of the restrictions, however, is squarely aimed at cis-gendered women and that is what I am referring to in this sentence.

6 Sex and the Black Christian girl

34. Contemporary regional forms of AAVE, principally in the greater Atlanta, GA area, sometimes use "nasty" to describe something as exceptional or outstanding. This is very similar to reappropriation of the term "bad".

35. This is, of course, is not inclusive of those suffering from mental disorders which hinder impulse control. And I am specifically talking about sexual acts between consenting bodies.

36. Not the real names of the brothers.

37. Not his real name.

7 The road to Queerville

38. My grandfather died suddenly while I was home for spring break in 1999.

39. I experienced a number of health issues related to allergies that doctors could not figure out. One suggestion made to me was to stop taking my birth control pills which were of an unusually high dose. I started experiencing libido changes after I stopped that medication.

40. This UK documentary was directed by Brigid McFall and can be watched on the Channel 4 website.

41. According to the summary of the documentary on Channel 4's site: www.channel4.com/programmes/where-have-all-the-lesbians-gone/on-demand/72862-001

42. Some of us have the privilege of living out complicated sexual lives, whilst some live in more conservative contexts that are more socially constricted.

43. Years later, when the UK passed its own marriage equality act, Gillian and I went back to Annan and converted our civil partnership officially to marriage. Shirley was still there and presided over the change. I wore the same dress.

44. Scotland accepted electronic paperwork. In England, applications had to be made in person.

45. It was not until 2019 (Iqbal) that UK law changed to allow heterosexual couples to have non-religious civil unions.

46. I am the founder and owner of BB Naturals, a solutions-based brand catering for those with textured hair and sensitive skin.

8 Love as a mission

47. I was assigned "female" at birth (AFAB), and I identify as a woman, meaning I am cis-gendered. Not everyone assigned a gender based on their biological sex at birth grow to identify with that gender. That makes them trans-gendered or non-binary.

48. My words here apply to those with medical conditions where they experience disassociation or are declared mentally incapacitated, thus unable to understand their actions.

49. hooks, b., 2000. *All About Love: New Visions*. New York: Harper Perennial.

50. As was the case at a New York University dining hall during Black History Month in 2018 Astor.

51. I hate this term, not the least because it has legitimized what should be seen as economic failure and financial insecurity. This expectation to have a "side-hustle" legitimizes that fact that the cost of living has exceeded the rise of wages. Furthermore, the "side hustle" economy like transport services, food delivery, and so on, has normalized labor exploitation.

Discussion questions

1. Are there unifying aspects of the Black American experience? If so, what are they? What are the experiences which may be regional?

2. What are the ways in which sexual education is tied to maintaining patriarchy? How does gender, race, and sexual identity shape sexual education?

3. In what ways are women-identified people's bodies regarded as public "property"?

4. How is shame shaped by religious values (not limited to Christianity)? Which religions promote shame most? Which religions navigate away from sexual shame?

5. Is it possible for love and capitalism to co-exist? Why or why not? What are some examples of co-existence?

References

American Crime Story. (2016). "The Race Card". [TV Series]. FX Network.

Astor, M. (2018). Black History Month Menu at N.Y.U.: Kool-Aid, Watermelon and Controversy. *New York Times*. [Online]. Available at www.nytimes.com/2018/02/21/nyregion/nyu-black-history-month.html [Accessed 15 February 2023].

Atlanta. (2022). "Trini 2 de bone". [TV Series]. FX Network.

Baldwin, J. (1965). Pin Drop Speech at Harvard University. [Speech]. Available at www.youtube.com/watch?v=NUBh9GqF U3A [Accessed 17 February 2023].

Brookings Institute. (2003). Neighborhood 10: Ten Strategies for a Stronger Washington. [Report]. Available at www.brookings. edu/wp-content/uploads/2016/06/20030417_revitalizingdc_w illiams.pdf . [Accessed 17 February 2023].

CNN.com. (2016). CNN Exit Poll 2016. [Online]. Available at https://edition.cnn.com/election/2016/exit-polls/president/national-results [Accessed 12 October 2022].

Crenshaw, K.W. (1991). Mapping the Margins: Intersectionality, Identity Politics, and Violence Against Women of Color. In *The public nature of private violence*. (pp. 93–118). Oxford: Routledge.

Dubois, W.E.B. (2009 (1903)). *The Souls of Black Folk*. New York: Oxford University Press.

Durr, M. (2015). What is the Difference between Slave Patrols and Modern Day Policing? Institutional Violence in a Community of Color. *Critical Sociology*, 41(6), 873–879. https://doi.org/10.1177/0896920515594766

Freire, P. (1970). *Pedagogy of the Oppressed*. New York: "Continuum Press.

Glickman, C. (2012). "Queer is a Verb". In *Momentum: Making Waves in Sexuality, Feminism, and Relationships*. Tess Danesi, Dee Dennis, and Inara de Luna (eds.). Selected essays by 2012 (conference) speakers advocating change in current sexual dialogues. Available at https://new.charlieglickman.com/queer-is-a-verb/ . [Accessed 12 January 2023].

Hall, S. et al. (1982). Policing the Crisis: Mugging. In *The State and Law and Order*. London: Red Globe Press.

High on the Hog. (2021). [Documentary]. *Netflix*.

Hochschild, A. and Machung, A. (1989). *The Second Shift: Working Families and the Revolution at Home*. New York: Penguin Books.

Holifield, J. (2021). White House Initiative on Historically Black Colleges and Universities: Contributions Brief. [Report]. Available at https://sites.ed.gov/whhbcu/files/2021/01/HBCU-Contributions-Brief.pdf . [Accessed 15 February 2023].

hooks, bell. (2000). *All About Love: New Visions*. New York: Harper Collins.

Ikpi, B. (2019). *I'm Telling the Truth but I'm Lying*. New York: Harper Perennial.

Iqbal, N. 2019. Let's Keep it Civil…Met the First Couples Embracing Partnerships under the New Law. [Online] *The Guardian*. www.theguardian.com/uk-news/2019/dec/29/first-of-84000-couples-get-set-for-a-civil-partnership [Accessed 15 February 2023].

Judas and the Black Messiah. (2021). [Film]. Hollywood, CA: Shaka King.

Junn, J. (2016). Hiding in Plain Sight: White Women Vote Republican. *Politics of Color*. [Online]. Available at http://politicsofcolor.com/white-women-vote-republican/. [Accessed 17 February 2023].

Lorde, A.. (1982). Learning from the 60s. [Lecture]. www.blackp ast.org/african-american-history/1982-audre-lorde-learning-60s/ [Accessed 17 February 2023].

Morrison, T. 1994 *Playing in the Dark: Whiteness and the Literary Imagination*. Cambridge: Harvard University Press.

Morrow, R. and Ikpi, B. (2022). Episode #93, "The Big Payback, Cancer Attack". *This Too Much*. The Black Guy Who Tips Network. [Podcast]. Available at https://open.spotify.com/episode/2v0 0GHaFzDLSrPMFrYlpKh?si=V28Yq09VRD2fTGqMG2coWg . [Accessed 15 February 2017]

Neophytou, N. (2016). Katy Perry Comes Out to Try… [Tweet]. Available at https://twitter.com/NadiaNeophytou/status/796 190867564457984?ref_src=twsrc%5Etfw%7Ctwcamp%5Etwe etembed%7Ctwterm%5E796190867564457984%7Ct wgr%5E3692120d7417cafbe94b869def05470d8464cadc%7Ctw con%5Es1_c10&ref_url=https%3A%2F%2Fpeople.com%2Fem bed%3Furl%3Dhttps3A2F2Ftwitter.com2Ftwitter2Fstatus2F7 96190867564457984id%3Dmntl-sc-block_1-0-6-iframeopti ons%3De303Ddocld%3D6023584 [Accessed 17 February 2023].

Office of the Chief Medical Examiner (DC). (Unknown). A 30-Year Review of Homicides in the District of Columbia (19722002). Washington, D.C: Office of the Chief Medical Examiner, 2-17. [Report] Available at https://ocme.dc.gov/sites/default/files/dc/ sites/ocme/publication/attachments/APPENDIX%20A%20-%20 30%20year.pdf . [Accessed 17 February 2023].

Pew Research Center (2009). Dissecting the 2008 Electorate: The Most Diverse in History. Available at www.pewresearch.org/ hispanic/2009/04/30/dissecting-the-2008-electorate-most-dive rse-in-us-history/. [Accessed 17 February 2023].

Pow, K. (2018). Be Exactly Who You Are: Black Feminism in Volatile Political Realities. In: A. Johnson, R.J. Salisbury and B. Kamunge, eds., *The Fire Now: Anti-racist Scholarship in Times of Explicit Racial Violence*. London, UK: Zed Books, pp. 235–249.

Pow, K. (2021). *"The Woman Saying This is Black Like Us": Intersectionality and Black Women's Fandom and Intersectionality Discourse on Tumblr.* PhD. Birmingham City University. Available at www.open-access.bcu.ac.uk/13624/ [Accessed 17 February 2023].

Sandberg, S. (2013). *Lean In: Women, Work and the Will to Live.* New York: Random House, Inc.

Scandal. (2013). "It's Handled" [TV Series]. ABC Network.

Steele, D. (1989). *Star: A Novel.* New York: Random House, Inc.

Strauss, V. and Mathews, J. (2017). "Trump Moves Program on Historically Black Colleges into the White House". Available at www.washingtonpost.com/local/education/trump-moves-prog ram-on-historically-black-colleges-into-the-white-house/2017/ 02/28/64acd09c-fe04-11e6-8f41-ea6ed597e4ca_story.html

The Carters. (2018). Black Effect. *Everything Is Love.* [Online]. Sony Music Entertainment. Available at https://youtu.be/mLYKSGKE rX4. [Accessed 17 February 2023].

The L Word. (2005). "Labyrinth". [TV Series] Showtime. Available at https://youtu.be/ygc2mJA49Gk [Accessed 17 February 2023].

West, Crissle. (2014). Lemon Pepper Wings. [Podcast]. The Read. Loud Speakers Network. Available at https://soundcloud.com/ theread/lemon-pepper-wings . [Accessed 15 February 2023].

Where Have All the Lesbians Gone? (2022). [Documentary]. United Kingdom: McFall and Lentaigne. Available at www.channel4. com/programmes/where-have-all-the-lesbians-gone/on-dem and/72862-001 [Accessed 15 February 2023].

Recommended further reading

The Fire Now: Anti-racist Scholarship in Times of Racial Violence by Azeezat Johnson, Remi-Joseph Salisbury, and Beth Kamunge.

No Tea, No Shade: New Writings in Black Queer Studies by E. Patrick Johnson.

The Sovereignty of Quiet: Beyond Resistance in Black Culture by Kevin Quashie.

"The Woman Saying this is Black like us": Black Women's Fandom and Intersectionality Discourse on Tumblr, dissertation by Kadian Pow http://www.open-access.bcu.ac.uk/13624/.

Sula, by Toni Morrison.

Black Skin, White Masks, by Frantz Fanon.

Taking Up Space, the Black Girl's Manifesto for Change by Chelsea Kwakye and Ore Ogunbiyi.

Out of the House of Bondage, by Thavolia Glymph.

Beyond Respectability: The Intellectual Thought of Race Women by Brittney C. Cooper.

The Boundaries of Desire: A Century of Bad Laws, Good Sex and Changing Identities by Eric Berkowitz.

Being Black: Zen and the Art of Living with Fearlessness and Grace by Angel Kyodo Williams.

How Should A Person Be? by Sheila Heti.

High on the Hog: A Culinary Journey from Africa to America, by
   Jessica B. Harris.

Index

abortion, 93

Adams, Lynette, 43

adolescent identities, 90

adolescent sexual hormones, 100

adult film industry, 110

African American Alumni of
  Vassar College (AAAVC)
  organization, 26–27

African-Americans, 2

  alumnus of Sarah Lawrence
    College, 27

  culture, 40, 135, 137

  diaspora outside of
    America, 39

  financial entrepreneurship, 138

  life at school, 23

  Southern American life, 23

  study programs, 27

African-American Vernacular
  English (AAVE), 103n1, 117

Alderson Federal Prison
  Center, 71

All About Love (2012), 135

All My Children (soap opera), 131

American churches,
  denominations of, 18

American conservatism, 62

American culture, 16

American Dream, 19

American food, 9

American identity, 10

American masculinity, 63

American political
  polarization, 119

American politics, 25

American residency, 78

artificial hormones, 107

assigned "female" at birth
  (AFAB), 141n1

Atlanta (FX TV show), 58, 136

Baldwin, James, 65

BB Naturals, 125n9, 139–141

Benjamin Banneker Academic
  Senior High School, 18, 43–44

betraying the trust,
  consequences of, 108

Bible study group, 77

bigotry, European Christian
  influences of, 42

bipolar disorder, 3

birth control pills, 92, 107, 109, 124n2

bisexuality, 112

Black admittance, criteria for, 19

Black American culture, 23

artistic expression of, 136

Black Americans, 2, 117

Black baby boomer generation, 27

Black children

around white people, 39

doing free labor for racism, 41

Black criminality, 37

Black culture, 88, 136

Black Delta Sorority, 91

"Black Effect" song, 135

Black excellence, 46

Black Guy Who Tips, The, 78

Black humanity, 59

Black identity, 2

Black labor, 59

Black liberation, 55

Black lives, authenticity of, 137

Black neighborhood, 16

blackness

idea of, 15, 18–24

types of, 29

of universities, 22

Black people, 19, 46

American mythology of, 17

American Negro, 16

civil rights, 61

cultural authenticity, 19

as embodiment of criminality, 37

enrolment at PWIs, 27

pupils, 15

racial discrimination, in voting, 61

right to attend university in any state, 27

sociological concept of, 15

subjugation of, 23

teachers, 16

white people antipathy towards freedom of, 66

Black specialists, on Indian culture(s), 49

Black Student Unions (BSU), 27–28

Black women, 24, 43, 54, 58, 141

bodies of, 58

in casting off shame, 110

corporate success, 46

economic value of involuntary labor, 58

idea of gendered liberation, 46

job market limitations for, 105

service industry work, 58

Blake, Mr., 10

"Blue Ribbon" school, 18

"blue" video, 87

bodily pleasure, sense of, 94

British colonialism, legacy of, 42

British legal system, 122

Bush, George W., 97

Catholicism, 80

Chaka Khan song, 66

childcare services, 58, 130

Chocolate City, 40, 73

Christian campus group, 81

Christian fearmongering, 72–74

Christianity, 71, 74, 77, 80

   moral tenets of, 86

   White evangelical
      supremacist, 73

Christian monologues, 71

Christ, Jesus, 71

Church of England, 121

Church of God, 71

cis-gendered women, 84n7

civil partnership, 121

civil rights, 27, 61

Clark Atlanta University, 21

class-based society, 42

Clint Eastwood films, 56

Clinton, Bill, 63

cognitive behavioral therapy
   (CBT), 92

college sports institution, 21

color prejudice, 42

community college, 21

copulation, idea of, 85

Covid-19 pandemic, 32

Crenshaw, Kimberlé, 1

cultural anthropology, 105

cultural appropriation, 136

cultural transition, 13

Culture and Development
   program, 63

Dark Ages in Europe, 83

Defense of Marriage Act
   (DoMA), 119

dental insurance, 106

Different World, A (TV show), 20

dildo (sex toy), 109–111

domestic care-givers, 58

domestic labor, 33

double consciousness, notion
   of, 16, 39

drug trade, 74

Dubois, W.E.B., 16, 39

dyscalculia, 113

dyslexia, 113

education in schools,
    relationship- building, 98

emotional intelligence, 98

English language, 135

enslaved people, 67

ethics-based training, 52n5

evangelical churches, 71, 80

Facebook, 48, 62, 64

Falwell, Jerry, 73

fast food, 9

Fayetteville State University, 21

female sexuality, 112

feminism
    idea of gendered liberation, 46

    "second wave" of, 46

    spectrum of identity, 71

    whiteness of, 53–55

feminist leadership, 53

feminist movement, 53

    tenets of, 47

financial security, 51, 118

The Fire Now: Scholarship in Times
    of Explicit Racial Violence
    (2018), 61

food emporium, Chinese-run, 10

food preparation, 31

food shopping, 10

fraud, allegations of, 17

Freire, Paolo, 66

Friday Night Lights (TV show), 77

Fugitive Slave Act of 1850, 66

Fundamentalist Latter-Day Saints
    (FDLS), 82

gendered liberation, idea of, 46

gender identities, 13

gender imbalances, 55

gender-inclusive marriage,
    legalizing of, 120

General Hospital (soap opera), 131

generational divide, 115

Generation X, 106

Glickman, Charlie, 117

God's army, 71

Graduate Equivalent Diploma
    (GED), 52n3

Hall, Stuart, 37

Hampton University, 21

hardship scholarship, 28

healthcare industry, 55

health service business, 38

hetero-patriarchal power and
authority, 53

heterosexual identity, 112

heterosexuality, boundaries of,
117–118

higher education,
institutions of, 19

higher learning institutions, 19

High on the Hog (Netflix
documentary), 35n6

Hillman University, 20

Historically Black University or
College (HBCU), 19–20, 27–28

funding for, 35n4

White House Initiative on, 35n4

Historically White Institutions
(HWIs), 19

HIV/AIDS crisis, 72

fearmongering about, 97

Hochschild, Arlie Russell, 33

Hollywood, 131

homophobia, 97

homosexuality, scientific
legitimacy of, 116

house of bondage, 58–60

human corporate entities, 118

human reproductive
education, 97

identity, sense of, 54

Ikpi, Bassey, 3, 136

immigrants, 42–47

Immigration and Nationality
Act, 84n6

impending adulthood, anxiety
of, 33–34

imposter syndrome, 48

induction ceremonies, 60

industrial clean right, 106

in-state university system, 21

institutional patriarchal
system, 53

intellectual property rights, 136

intersectionality, concept of, 1

involuntarily celibate (InCels), 95

Jamaican tastes and cravings, 10

Jim Crow segregation, 58

job market, 105

Johnson, Lyndon B., 61, 63

"Just Say No" anti-drug
campaign, 72

Land of Opportunity, 42

Langley Park, Maryland, 10

Languages and Cultures of Asia, 105

law enforcement officers, 67

Lawrence, Sarah, 35n7

Lean Back™, 51

Lean In: Women, Work, and the Will to Lead (Sheryl Sandberg), 48

learning about sex, 95

Lee, Robert E., 23

lesbian

   lesbian sex, 111, 112–114

   versus queer people, 115–116

Longfellow Street, 8, 11

Lorde, Audre, 1–2

love

   and capitalism, 139–141

   as a commitment, 134–135

   Love's Lover, 127–131

   loving blackness, 135–139

low-income people, 106

L Word, The (Showtime's sapphic soap), 111–113, 133

marriage, "hetero- sanctity" of, 121

Marshall, Thurgood, 61

Mason-Dixon line, 22

Math Honor Society, 41

Media Boulevard, 111, 113

Medicaid, 106

melatonin, effect of, 89

mental health

   conversation, 106

   intervention, 106

misogynoir, 46

monogamous marriage, 82

Montgomery County, 17

Morrison, Toni, 41

Morrow, Rod, 78, 136

murder capital, 73

Murphy, Ryan, 18

non-American Blacks, 29

non-believers, lives of, 83

non-Black people, 17

Obama, Barack, 120–121

Obergefell v. Hodges, 119

one's self, 16

organizational culture, 67

outsider-ness, idea of, 42

oxytocin, post-orgasmic release of, 89

parent-teacher conferences, 60

patriarchal order, 32

patriarchal supremacy, 45

people of color, 17, 63, 66, 112

Perry, Katy, 62–63

personal care, 51

Pleasure Chest, 110

policing

   culture of, 67

   institution of, 66

Policing the Crisis: Mugging, The State and Law and Order (1982), 37

pornography

   exposure to, 86, 94, 97, 131

   industry, 95

Porter, Bette, 133

post-coital tristesse (post-sex sadness), 88

power, colonial sense of, 46

Predominately White Institution (PWI), 19, 20, 24, 47

   Black student enrolment at, 27

   East Coast PWIs, 27

   history of Black activism at, 28

pregnancy

   cycle of, 89

   fear of, 107

Prince Georges County, 17

protestant Christian values, 69

puberty, 85–88

public economy, 57

public-school education, 15

queer people

   as a choice, 116–119

   versus lesbian and bisexual, 115–116

   people of color, 112

   "Queer is a Verb" essay, 117

queer sex, 92

"Rabbit" toy. *see* dildo (sex toy)

racial discrimination, in voting, 61

racial disparity, 72

racial ethnic groups, 68n8

racial exclusion, practice of, 19

racial hierarchy, 38

racial statistics, 64

racism, 46

rape, 58

Read, The, 54

recruitment, of Black professors, 27

Red Apple Market, 10

Red Delicious apple, 9

religious worker, 78, 84n6

reproductive care, 83

Republican party, 63

residential areas, racial segregation of, 16

Rhee, Michelle, 16

right-to-life arguments, 70

right to terminate a pregnancy, protection of, 82

Rockville Church of God, 17, 64

Rockville, Maryland, 17

Rodham-Clinton, Hillary, 63

Roe v. Wade, 60–61, 82

romantic fantasy, 131

romantic love stories, 131

Safeway grocery store, 9–10

same-gender sexual relationships, 112

same sex marriage, ban on, 121

Sandberg, Sheryl, 48

Scandal (TV show), 2, 45

scholarship money, 20

Seinfeld (TV show), 25

self-determination, 1

self-identity, 13

self-improvement campaign, 12

self, sense of, 13

sense of responsibility, 32

sex

   as a disease, 95–98

   learning about, 95

   pleasure principle, 72

queer sex, 92

"sin" of, 82

Sex and the City (television show), 110

sex information, mechanics and aesthetics of, 98

sexual abuse, 131

sexual activity

   attractive *versus* attraction, 98–103

   avoidance of sex, 90

   with boys, 89

   female orgasm, 110

   guilt and shame around self-pleasure, 94

   masturbation, 88–91, 94

   pleasure–shame cycle, 89

   pornography, exposure to, 86

   post-orgasmic disgust, 94

   queer sex, 92

   rape, 58

   self-induced orgasms, 110

   and sense of shame, 92

   sexual intercourse, 85

   sexual pressure from boys, 92

sexual and romantic relationship, 111

sexual attractiveness, 98–103

sexual autonomy, right to, 46

sexual desire, 88

sexual disease, 97

sexual education, 97

sexual engagement, 97

sexual fantasies, 91, 94

sexual health, concern for, 95

sexual identity, 91, 110–111

sexual impropriety, 17

sexual intercourse,
  mechanics of, 98

sexuality, hetero and homo
  polarities of, 117

sexual proclivity, 116

sexual relationship, for
  transactional gain, 45

sexual tourists, 112

shame, idea of, 97

"sin" of sex, 82

situational sexuality, 112

slave-holding states, political
  representation of, 67

Smithsonian's National Museum
  of Natural History, 122

social and economic security, 25

social interactions, 27

social media, 19, 62, 99

Souls of Black Folk, The (1903), 16

Southern Black College Tour, 24

space-time continuum, 70

state sanctioned law
  enforcement, 37

state universities, 26

Steele, Danielle, 24

street harassment, 99

Sunday meal, 30

Super Woman, 57

Supreme Court of the United
  States (SCOTUS), 82

teenage identity, 93

teenage love, idea of, 92

teen pregnancy

  fate worse than death, 91–95

  rise in rates of, 72

This Too Much (media review
  podcasts), 136

Thornton, Reverend, 76

TikTok video, 118

"town-gown" relations, 74

transculturation, space of, 22

Trini 2 de Bone, 58

Trump, Donald, 35n4, 61–66

tuition and fees, 28

Twitter, 13, 19, 62, 119, 127

two-ness, sense of, 16

United States Holocaust Memorial Museum (USHMM), 114

Education department of, 48

Law Enforcement and Society ethics training program, 47

universities, blackness of, 22

University of Chicago, 109

University of North Carolina-Chapel Hill (UNC), 21

University of Pennsylvania, 106

University of Wisconsin-Madison, 106

US Department of Education

National Blue-Ribbon School award, 35n3

Vassar College in Poughkeepsie, New York, 24–30, 105

violence, threat of, 109

virginity of a girl, 90

Voting Rights Act of 1965, 61

wage-earning jobs, 33

wages, women's, 57–58

war on drugs, 72

Washington, DC, 99, 121

wealth inequality, 118

West African food traditions, 35n6

West, Crissle, 54

Where Have All the Lesbians Gone? (Channel 4 documentary), 115

white capitalist patriarchal supremacy, 135–136

white people

antipathy towards Black people's freedom, 66

existentialism of, 58

hetero-patriarchal supremacy, 65

racial colorblindness, 60

taboo topics, 60

white spaces, Black faces in, 15–18

white supremacy, 41, 58, 138

hetero-patriarchal, 65

notion of, 19

white women, 63

Williams, Anthony, 16

Wisconsin, 31

woman's punishment for sexual autonomy, 83

women-identified persons, 115

women's bodies, notion of, 13

women's liberation, from the domestic space, 57

women's lifelong service, to the family, 33

working-class people, 42

Printed in the USA
CPSIA information can be obtained
at www.ICGtesting.com
JSHW062024230823
47038JS00005BA/295

9 781915 271457